SECRET SUPPERS

Rogue Chefs and Underground Restaurants
in Warehouses, Townhouses, Open Fields,
and Everywhere in Between

Jenn Garbee

SASQUATCH BOOKS
SEATTLE

For my husband, Kevin; wine; and chocolate
(in no particular order).

Printed in the United States of America
Published by Sasquatch Books
Distributed by PGW/Perseus
15 14 13 12 11 10 09 08   9 8 7 6 5 4 3 2 1

Cover illustration/photograph: © Stockbyte photography/veer.com
Cover design: Rosebud Eustace
Interior design and composition: Brad Greene/Greene Design
Interior photographs: Jenn Garbee (except background image on pages viii–1, 26–27, 48–49, 76–77,
    102–103, 128–129, 152–153, 174–175, 198–199, 224–225, and back cover: Stephan Szpak-Fleet/
    Texture of Europe/www.sxc.hu)

Library of Congress Cataloging-in-Publication Data
Garbee, Jenn.
Secret suppers : rogue chefs and underground restaurants in
warehouses, townhouses, open fields, and everywhere in between / Jenn Garbee.--1st ed.
    p. cm.
Includes index.
ISBN-13: 978-1-57061-546-7
ISBN-10: 1-57061-546-2
1. Suppers. 2. Dinners and dining. 3. Cookery. I. Title.
TX738.G37 2008
641.5′38--dc22
                    2008022780

Sasquatch Books
119 South Main Street, Suite 400
Seattle, WA 98104
(206) 467-4300
www.sasquatchbooks.com
custserv@sasquatchbooks.com

CONTENTS

INTRODUCTION

It all started a few years ago when I attended an underground dinner in San Francisco on assignment for the *Los Angeles Times*. As I sat on a floor cushion in the volunteer host's dusty attic, munching sweet potato and Peruvian pepper–slathered plantain chips with thirty other quasi-guests (all paying for the privilege to dine there), it struck me as a decidedly simple—and logical—Internet-age alternative to classic entertaining, a way to meet new people while enjoying (in theory) a good meal. And it forever changed the way I think about home entertaining versus restaurant dining.

So what exactly is an underground restaurant?

It's the first question I'm invariably asked and the hardest to answer. The more dinners I attended, the more I (reluctantly) concluded that there isn't a clear definition. Although true that most rely heavily on the Internet to spread the word and filter potential guests to their RSVP-required (but not necessarily invitation-only) events, the similarities end there. My answer typically begins with a description of what an underground restaurant is not: it's not a standard dinner party with a few unknown faces around the table; it's not a group of friends and acquaintances who split the cost of dinners at rotating homes (otherwise known as a classic supper club); it's not a brick-and-mortar, fully licensed restaurant (which is not to say all undergrounds are illegal; catering licenses can come in handy).

The easiest way to understand the underground movement is to talk to the chefs behind these semisecret dining clubs and their guests. So that's exactly what I did.

Finding underground restaurants was relatively easy; choosing which to attend was not. I wanted restaurants that were diverse not only in type (from small, twelve-person events to roving events with more than one hundred guests) but also in geography (big city to small town). Perhaps not surprisingly, finding them in large metropolitan cities was as simple as using an Internet search engine; midsize cities and suburban areas required phone calls to local chefs, chats with food bloggers, and plain old good luck.

Who exactly is behind this underground restaurant movement? The participants are as diverse as their restaurants, from big-city chefs to small-town home cooks and everything in between. Some, like Hal Jasa of Underground, Inc., are former professional chefs fed up with the limitations of the restaurant world where the bottom line often overshadows creative cooking.

Others, such as HUSH chef Anne Horstmann of Washington, D.C., are young chefs who will work as line cooks and sous chefs for years before they'll be able to express their culinary creativity as head chefs . . . except in the underground world. Still others, including Jim Denevan of Outstanding in the Field, began hosting dinners to educate the public about food choices—farmers market produce versus grocery store imports—and became successful business owners. For these food industry professionals, the underground dining world is an opportunity to own, manage, and cook at their own restaurants without the high dollar investment typically required to open a brick-and-mortar establishment.

Some underground chefs, including James Stolich of San Francisco's CookWithJames, the Whisk & Ladle crew, and Robyn of Caché in Seattle, are avid home cooks who enjoy the challenge and opportunity to be chef-for-the-day: cooking for a limited number of people in a private environment. Talented home cooks turned underground restaurateurs are often encouraged by their dinner guests to go a step further—catering or private chef work as Robyn has, or trying other food outlets, such as James's foray into television cooking programs.

Others get into the underground restaurant game for personal reasons. For Mike Sherwood, Sub Rosa is essentially a creative online home page, a window into his Dundee, Oregon, life. Scott Beattie and Ross Hallett hold their wine country undergrounds so they can taste top wines; Hannah Calvert of Supper Underground in Austin, Texas, read an article about an underground restaurant and thought "it sounded like fun and a great way to meet people"; and Josh Loeb launched Farmers Market Wednesdays with the goal of opening a real restaurant.

As for who attends and what the ten underground restaurants profiled in *Secret Suppers* are really like, you'll have to read the book. By the time this book is published, however, many of these undergrounds will have changed dramatically. And that's half the fun of attending—it's never the same twice.

COOK WITH JAMES

~

Dear Friends,

I am very pleased to announce an upcoming special supper club dinner Saturday, August 18th, 2007. I have a few seats left so please book quickly!

This summer has been very kind to us in the way of excellent produce. Naturally I never know the menu until the day I hit the market but here are some dishes that have been coming out of my kitchen recently.

See you at the table or maybe the market!

Best, James

~

CHAPTER 1

James Stolich's wife, Pia, is chatting with guests in the parlor of their San Francisco Victorian, her hands dancing through the air, eyes as big as saucers. She's swooning in syrupy Italian-soaked English about spring peas. Or maybe she said pecorino cheese. It's hard to understand from the kitchen, where I'm watching James carefully drizzle aged balsamico and *olio nuovo* on roasted baby beets with burrata cheese, the first of six courses.

"*Il primo,*" James says, smiling.

Once a month James, a thirty-six-year-old advertising executive, and Pia, an Italian teacher and designer from Naples, Italy, host elaborate Italian dinner parties for a dozen guests in their Cole Valley home. Only they're not exactly dinner parties. Guests here request reservations via e-mail and pay for the privilege of dining in the Stolich home. And that privilege doesn't come cheap. Recently, James raised the price to $100 per person, not including wine.

Tonight's guests, a mix of James and Pia's friends and people they've never met, are perfectly happy to fork over the funds. In fact, many have asked James to host the dinners more often. "He's an excellent cook, a true chef," one guest declares. "Better than many of the restaurants in town," adds a friend who has dined here several times, both as a paying customer and as an invited guest at one of James and Pia's private dinner parties. That's quite a statement in San Francisco, a city with a seemingly endless roster of first-rate restaurants.

"Would you like an espresso?" asks James, peeking at the Bolognese sauce that's been simmering on his canary yellow Lacanche stove since early morning. "I just got a new machine this week. I haven't even tested it out yet."

Normally I'd be clamoring to taste an espresso from a La Spaziale machine, one of the best, and most expensive, home models available. One of these beauties will set you back a couple thousand dollars and take over a hefty chunk of prime kitchen counter real estate.

But I'm completely enraptured by James's stove. Lacanche is the Mercedes of stovetops, built for power and longevity, but able to handle the most delicate of cooking. I've rarely seen one outside a professional kitchen, or outside Europe for that matter. It's regal, yet unassuming and surprisingly compact—two traditional gas burners plus a third covered by a cast-iron simmer plate—considering the quantity of dishes James is cooking tonight. And for fourteen people, no less.

"Oh, yeah; Michael managed to find that stove for me," he says nonchalantly as he hands me a perfectly pulled espresso with its telltale caramel head. Michael is James Beard–nominated chef Michael Tusk, the chef-owner of Quince restaurant.

The espresso is excellent. "The Spaziale is fully plumbed into the sink and remains ready for action twenty-four hours a day," James says matter-of-factly. Still, I find it hard to believe he is willing to dedicate half his tiny countertop to caffeine. But then again, no proper Italian would go through the day without *un magnifico* shot of espresso. And James isn't much different from any other kitchen-savvy Italian expatriate with a palate more in tune with Old Country cuisine than with the Italian-American fare served stateside. Only he isn't Italian—and he wasn't always so keen on cooking.

James grew up in Carmel-by-the-Sea, the California resort town known more for its golf courses than for its local cuisine. His first bite of gotta-learn-to-cook food didn't pass his lips until he was a Spanish literature graduate student in Madrid. But it wasn't any Ferrán Adrià-inspired foie gras foam, cumin gel, and eau de bacon gas that hit his culinary soft spot. Adrià's molecular gastronomy experiments had nothing on the dishes Mamá Lola Reparaz, his host mother, turned out nightly.

Mamá Lola wooed James with simple Spanish home cooking: *pollo con naranjas* (crispy roasted chicken stuffed with oranges), *tortillas de patata* (potato omelets), and his favorite afternoon snack, *croquetas de jamón Serrano* (fried milk and Serrano ham squares). Mamá Lola sent James home with a handwritten three-hundred-page cookbook filled with favorite family recipes, whimsical drawings, and motherly advice penned in the margins. She'd already hand copied the book twice, one for each of her children. A third for James? *¡Por supuesto!*

The book sat in James's San Francisco kitchen cabinet for seven years, untouched. He was too busy with a booming high-tech career and wooing Pia, his soon-to-be bride.

On September 11, 2001, James's life changed forever. The world turned upside down, the stock market crashed, and the company James worked for went out of business. He found himself sitting on the couch with the TV remote in hand, unemployed . . . and hungry.

"I was addicted to the Food Network," James sheepishly admits. "No, really addicted. But this was back when they had chefs like Wolfgang Puck who were teaching how to make good, classic dishes, not those people they have on there now. Wolfgang just looked so happy cooking. I figured I should give it a try."

James taped an episode featuring roasted Chilean sea bass with braised escarole and cannellini beans. He watched it over and over, studied Wolfgang's technique, and whipped it up for Pia that evening.

"Actually, it was good, really good," he recalls. "But back then my plating skills still needed a lot of work."

Fast forward a year to James's new career in advertising and an insatiable addiction to the stovetop. James had already plowed through his favorite cookbooks, including Mamá Lola's tome, and was cooking his way across Italy via Pia's family recipes. But cooking from recipes was one thing; he wanted to understand food from the eyes of a great chef, to see an ingredient and instinctively know what to pair it with and how to prepare it without pulling out instructions.

Fritz Streiff, a neighbor with a gold medal cooking pedigree from Chez Panisse, became his cooking mentor. "It just sort of happened; the two of us started hanging out, talking about food," recalls James.

Fritz enlightened James on all things Alice (as in Alice Waters): how to pick the perfect peach, how to keep the flavor at the forefront, how to fuss with nature as little as possible—a drizzle of muscat and a sprinkle of pistachios, perhaps a quick roast in the oven.

James was hungry for more, so one afternoon he called Michael, whom he didn't know at the time, and asked if he could intern in the Quince kitchen.

Free labor in a professional kitchen isn't always tops on a chef's must-have list. Untrained hands can ruin a dish . . . and the restaurant's reputation. And without formal training or restaurant experience, James wasn't exactly a hot commodity. But he was focused and meticulous, took direction well, and was eager to learn. Michael handed him an apron.

It was those eight months at Quince that turned James on to the idea of starting CookWithJames. He learned kitchen basics—how to properly dice vegetables, butterfly meat, poach an egg. But he also learned to make meltingly tender spinach gnocchi and crisp, juicy *carciofi alla Romana* (suckling pig).

At home Pia was his solo dinner guest. It's ironic, she recalls, that when they first met she did all the cooking: *palle di riso* (Neapolitan rice croquettes), *melanzane a scapece* (marinated eggplant), *bucatini sformato* (baked bucatini). These days she rarely sets foot in the kitchen, except for an espresso. Not that she's complaining. "He is so good at it, and it's his relaxation, so why interfere?" she says with a wink.

But there's a limit to how much food two people can eat.

James considered cooking professionally, but he didn't want the hassle and expense of opening a restaurant. And although inviting friends over to share in his elaborate feasts was satisfying, it was also expensive. He isn't the type to make lasagna and call it dinner. He pulls out all the stops, sparing no expense—to the tune of $400 on ingredients for a six-course dinner for twelve, not including wine.

The solution? Charge your friends.

"What is it you want me to do next, trim the pork?" asks Joseph in lilting French-accented English as he surveys the handwritten menu scribbled on a piece of scratch paper above the stove. Joseph has been here since noon. He's the volunteer kitchen assistant, a neighbor and longtime friend—the only person James trusts to help with the last-minute dinner preparations.

Joseph learned to cook in his native Brittany: *Coquilles St. Jacques* (creamed scallops), *gigot d'agneau* (lamb with rosemary), *cotriade Bretonne* (fish stew). When he immigrated to San Francisco thirty years ago, he opened a French bistro, the first of several successful restaurants.

He pulls a Prather Ranch pork shoulder for the *Brasato di Maiale alla Pugliese* (braised pork in the style of Puglia) from the fridge and clears a space on the butcher-block table in the corner, whistling softly as he works.

Joseph isn't simply comfortable in the kitchen; he's content. Trimming meat, sautéing artichokes, stoking the fireplace grill are his relaxation. "I could retire—really I am retired now that the last restaurant sold—but then if I admitted that, what would I do with myself?" he asks.

At CookWithJames, putting together the proper guest list is essential. With dinners only once every six weeks and a full week of late-night post-workday preparations, James has no room—or patience—for disgruntled guests. Twelve is the ideal number: enough appreciative palates to justify the days of preparation required, but not too many that the quality of the food, and the guest experience, suffers.

Occasionally, James will squeeze in a few extra chairs around great-grandmother Stolich's dining room table, like the two he added for his Prather Ranch meat purveyor, Doug Stonebraker, and his wife. "I try to include some of the people who provide the meal in the meal," says James.

Tonight, like most evenings, several guests are Pia and James's friends: two expatriate Italians, a couple of students from the Italian course Pia teaches at a local university, a friend who travels to Italy with the couple. The rest are a hodgepodge of online fans and curious foodies who heard about the dinners via James's Web site, press coverage, or word of mouth. Occasionally, James will pick up a dinner guest from his local hangouts— like the thirty-year-old doctor turned Medjool date peddler—("I just couldn't stay away from the family business")—who will be here tonight. He overheard James chatting about an upcoming dinner at the neighborhood coffee shop.

"Hey, it sounded like fun, something to check out, so I asked if I could come," says Barcelona, aka Barse to his friends. Sure, why not invite yourself to dinner at the home of someone you've never met? You're paying, so you should be able to attend if you'd like to.

Not exactly.

James is quick to point out that CookWithJames is a private underground restaurant—meaning he ultimately chooses who comes and who doesn't. You can't simply e-mail a reservation request and expect an invitation to dinner. James likes to get to know potential dinner guests via e-mail exchanges or, in the case of Barse, through a personal meeting.

A few weeks before each dinner, James sends an e-mail to his fan club of two hundred (and growing), announcing the upcoming date. It's not a huge list, but with only twelve seats per dinner, reservations fill quickly. The e-mail doesn't reveal what dishes will be served—that's yet to be determined depending on produce availability at the farmers market, although James usually chooses one ingredient to feature. All that's left to do is sit back and wait for James's reply.

Even with a double espresso in hand, James isn't a morning person. But on CookWithJames Saturdays, he's already hit the farmers market and is halfway into the Bolognese sauce by 8 AM. He's been preparing for tonight's dinner since Wednesday—making veal stock, slow-roasting tomatoes, and adjusting the seasoning on the sun-dried tomatoes and olives that have been curing in the pantry for weeks. He's a methodical planner, careful to leave plenty of time for shopping and cooking.

Tonight's feature ingredient is grass-fed beef from Prather Ranch, a top-quality (and über-expensive) purveyor. Every course—except the beet and burrata salad—features Prather Ranch lamb or beef.

The doorbell rings. It's Rhonda, a friend and local antique dealer (we're talking $3,000 chairs, not your aunt's hand-me-downs) who lives a few blocks down the street. She's toting half a dozen vases from her home collection and a cardboard box full of spring tulips. She gives Pia a kiss and heads straight to the dining room table, apparently in a hurry to get back home and change her clothes for dinner.

"Oh, no—I'm not coming to dinner tonight. I have plans," she says, poking tulips into the moss-filled vases. "Just wanted to bring by some flowers so the dinner is lovely."

Joseph lights the fireplace in the dining room and looks at his watch. Pia programs the iPod to Italian opera and glances in the mirror.

"James, what's on the menu again? Do we need steak knives? And how many forks?" Pia yells from the silverware cabinet.

The grandfather clock strikes eight. The guests will be here any minute.

Barse sets his motorcycle helmet in the hallway and saunters into the kitchen, where James is sprinkling sea salt and *olio nuovo* on roasted cashews. "Hey, man, those look good! Can I try one?" he asks as he hands James a container of Medjool dates from his family farm.

The dates will come in handy. For all the attention James gives to the six courses, dessert is rarely one of them. A couple of hunks of perfectly ripe cheese and a few squares of premium dark chocolate are all he can muster. "By the time I get to dessert, I'm just not interested anymore," he says. "And sweets aren't really my thing."

And if it's not his thing, James doesn't make it. It's his house, after all.

While we're chatting in the kitchen about the finer points of California dates (sweet Medjools versus mild Empress and delicate Deglets), Don and his wife, both students in Pia's Italian class, arrive with their daughter

Hillary. A recent college graduate and culinary student, Hillary read the menu and "just had to come. It sounded so authentic Italian, and I'm dying to study the cooking over there," she says, glancing at her dad.

This is a timely bunch. It's barely ten minutes after eight and all the guests have arrived. Not that I'm particularly surprised. Guests tend to be prompt at underground dinners—presumably because they're paying and want to get their money's worth. But unlike many underground diners, these guests, even ones who aren't friends of Pia and James, have brought gifts for the hosts: a bottle of artisan vinegar, a homemade jam, imported Italian olives.

The guests congregate in the living room, chatting over appetizers in front of the large bay window while watching the sun set behind meticulously restored, candy-colored Victorian homes. James sets down a large platter loaded with craggy chunks of Parmigiano-Reggiano, thinly rolled slices of prosciutto di Parma, Paul Bertolli salami, and the roasted cashews.

Doug and his wife are politely listening to Pia's Italian expatriate friends expound on the best, and worst, Italian restaurants in town.

"Honestly, we don't get out much," says Doug. "I'm always at our farmers market stand at the crack of dawn, so it limits our evenings. It's nice to sit down to dinner, meet new people."

Across the living room, a thirty-year-old philosophy major turned Internet executive is expounding on the finer points of artisan salami with two fortyish women, a psychologist and a winery public relations executive, while an aesthetician and her boyfriend chat about their hometowns.

"It's time for the traditional Prosecco toast. Let's all go out on the front porch," announces James, a bottle of bubbly in hand.

We head outside and James whips out a three-foot-long antique Napo-leonic sword—a bizarre scene for the neighbors, no doubt. He pulls the sword from its sheath, places it against the cork, gives it a firm swipe, and *bam!* The bottle pops open.

We all cheer and clap. It's a cheesy trick, but somehow James pulls it off. The Prosecco makes the rounds, and we head back inside for more nibbling and chatting. Pia flutters from group to group topping off our glasses, beaming as we rave over James's cashews.

The kitchen counter is crammed with a dozen plates topped with small mounds of field greens. Joseph spoons ruby red baby beets onto each plate and James follows with a slice of fresh burrata cheese. The cheese, fresh mozzarella stretched thin and stuffed with unfinished mozzarella curd and heavy cream, is from Italian cheese maker Vito Girardi in Southern California. Until Girardi started making it, burrata was difficult to find in the United States because of its extremely short shelf life—only two to three days. It's those kinds of lesser-known Italian ingredients that James likes to use for his dinners.

"*Il primo* is served; please find a seat," announces James as the clock strikes nine.

James sits in the chair closest to the kitchen; Pia takes the seat across from him. It's refreshing to see James and Pia at the table chatting with their guests and enjoying the meal, just like you'd imagine they'd do if they had invited you to dinner.

At a typical dinner party, guests not only expect their hosts to sit at the dinner table but would be offended—or at a minimum uncomfortable—if they didn't. In the underground dining world, however, the hosts typically act as both kitchen crew and servers. It's often a matter of necessity. If you're charging for dinner in your home—or anywhere—your guests expect the food to be perfectly cooked and the wineglasses always filled, much like a real restaurant.

But without the hosts at the table, it's a glaring reminder that you're a paying customer, not a true guest, no matter how underground restaurateurs try to convince you otherwise.

James and Joseph excuse themselves to prepare the second course, lamb riblets with mint and lemon pesto. James whisks fresh mint with olive oil to make a quick sauce, while Joseph slices the ribs and places two on each plate. With most of the prep work done in advance, it takes only ten minutes to get the second course—and James and Joseph—to the table.

"Wow, this lamb is amazing," says Barse between mouthfuls. "It doesn't have that heavy lamb taste that I don't like. Good work, James."

"You should really get into catering," suggests Hillary.

James lingers to chat for a few minutes before disappearing into the kitchen. Joseph gets up to clear the plates, and several guests instinctively

get up to help. Pia opens a couple more bottles of red table wine—Italian, of course—and turns up the Pavarotti.

Up next is *bruschetta di carcofi* (artichoke bruschetta). James announces each dish by its proper Italian name, followed by an English description. "Iacopi Farms has the best baby artichokes this year, so I wanted to highlight their flavor with a simple preparation. They're sautéed in a little olive oil and reduced white wine, sprinkled with Fleur de Sel, and spooned over toasted garlic bread," he explains.

The artichokes are delicious, perfectly tender and tasting of spring. I try not to clear my plate—we still have four courses to go—but I manage to polish off every bite.

The sauce for the fourth course, *pasta alla Bolognese* (pasta with tomato meat sauce), has been simmering since early morning. It's Pia's brother Pepi's recipe, slightly tweaked by James. One of her Italian friends is from Bologna, so we're all anxious—including James—to see what he thinks of Pepi's version.

We all watch as he takes a bite.

"*Bellisimo!*"

"No, really, tell me what you think," says James.

"It's good, really good. Lightly sauced, but flavorful—that's the key." James looks relieved. He gives full credit to the Prather Ranch ground beef.

"There's more?" Doug whispers to his wife. "It's almost midnight. I'm stuffed, and I've got to be at the market in six hours."

The Italians at the end of the table don't look fazed. They're just getting a second wind.

Joseph has been tinkering with the antique Tuscan grill in the dining room fireplace for twenty minutes, trying to get it hot enough to grill the *bistecca alla Fiorentina* (grilled Florentine steaks). James peeks out of the kitchen to check on his progress. "Joseph, are those steaks about ready to hit the fire?"

For the rest of us, it's a good excuse to get up from the table and stretch our legs after three hours of nonstop eating. I'm starting to regret polishing off that bruschetta.

Joseph tosses a handful of wild leeks on the grill and they flame up, causing a round of oohs and aahhs from the onlookers. Next, James puts two small Prather Ranch hanger steaks and two eight-ounce sirloins onto the grill, cooking them for a minute or two per side until they're medium rare. Those four steaks set him back a good $80, about three times what James could have spent on decent meat. But decent isn't what he's after.

James pulls the steaks off the grill and slices them thin enough to serve two slices of each cut to all fourteen guests. They are fantastic, with a big, beefy flavor. And the perfect quantity.

"Wow, this really tastes like steak," says Barse. "Don't think I've ever tasted steak like this before."

It's 1:30 in the morning when James sets the final savory course in front of us, a *Brasato di Maiale alla Pugliese* (braised pork shoulder, Puglia style). It very well could be the best dish of the evening—a succulent, tender, fall-apart mess with a delicate flavor that's somewhere between a pot roast and slow-cooked barbecue. But we're all too stuffed to manage more than a bite.

Now I understand why James doesn't serve dessert.

Half an hour later, James brings out the dates and a cheese platter: an oozy, perfectly ripe goat's milk robiola, a pungent Gorgonzola, and a hard sheep's milk cheese.

"James, I'm really sorry, but I have *got* to go to bed," says a groggy-eyed Doug. "It's well past my bedtime."

At a restaurant Doug might have left hours ago. But at a small, intimate underground restaurant like CookWithJames, there's the sense that it would be impolite to leave early.

No one else looks like they're going home anytime soon, so I grab a seat in the living room and try to look perky. They all commented on what a unique experience this was—how much they enjoyed getting to know new people in a home environment. Mainly, they can't stop raving about the food. I have to agree. The food was fantastic: simple Italian cooking served at home, just the way it should be. But I still don't understand exactly what drives James to throw such elaborate—and time-consuming—dinners. No matter how much you love to cook and entertain, it's a lot of work for a couple hundred bucks.

"Ultimately, I hope it will help me get my own television series. I have done some filming in conjunction with the dinners . . . and I really want to teach people my style of cooking."

Dinner parties this good can't last forever.

RECIPES

Burrata with Roasted Red and Yellow Baby Beets and Mixed Greens

James recommends substituting a good-quality buffalo mozzarella if you cannot find fresh burrata. Remember to remove the cheese from the refrigerator 1 hour prior to serving to bring it to room temperature.

Serves 8 as a first course

2 pounds baby red and yellow beets

3 tablespoons water

1 pound fresh burrata or buffalo mozzarella cheese

1 pound mixed baby greens, washed and spun dry

10 mint leaves, finely chopped

½ cup best-quality extra-virgin olive oil, preferably *olio nuovo*

1 teaspoon aged balsamic vinegar (optional)

Kosher or coarse-grain sea salt

Freshly cracked pepper

Preheat the oven to 425°. Cut the tips off the tops and bottoms of the beets and discard the greens. Scrub the beets under cold running water to remove any soil. Place the beets in a 9- by 13-inch glass baking dish, sprinkle with 3 tablespoons of water, and cover tightly with aluminum foil. Bake for 20 to 30 minutes or until beets are tender and easily pierced with a sharp knife. Remove from the baking dish and set aside to cool.

When the beets are cool, remove their skins by rubbing each beet with a paper towel. Remove any fibers or blemishes with a small knife; slice the beets into ¼-inch pieces. Cover with plastic wrap and refrigerate until ready to serve.

One hour before serving, remove the burrata and the beets from the refrigerator.

Slice the burrata into 8 wedges. Place a small handful of greens on each serving plate and top with a slice of burrata. Divide the beets among the plates and sprinkle with the mint leaves. Drizzle 1 table-spoon of the oil and a few drops of the vinegar over each salad. Sprinkle with the salt and pepper. Serve immediately.

Pepi's Pasta alla Bolognese (Pasta with Tomato Meat Sauce)

When James first tasted this Bolognese sauce at Pepi's house, he ate three enormous helpings, "something which is very unusual for me," he admits. He insists on using San Marzano canned tomatoes from Italy, available at well-stocked supermarkets. Look for full-fat (20 percent) ground beef from grass-fed cattle for a more flavorful result. The sauce takes 4 to 5 hours to prepare but can be made up to 2 days ahead and reheated.

Serves 6 to 8 as a pasta course

3 tablespoons olive oil

2 medium carrots, chopped into 1-inch pieces

1 large yellow onion, coarsely chopped

2 tablespoons plus ½ teaspoon kosher or coarse-grain sea salt, plus additional, divided

1 pound ground beef

1 28-ounce can San Marzano stewed tomatoes

¼ teaspoon freshly cracked pepper, plus additional, divided

1 pound tagliatelle or pappardelle egg pasta

About ¼ cup best-quality extra-virgin olive oil, preferably *olio nuovo*

Freshly grated Parmigiano-Reggiano cheese, for sprinkling

In a large stockpot with a lid, heat the olive oil over medium heat. Add the carrots, onion, and a pinch of salt. Sauté until the vegetables are soft but not browned, about 8 to 10 minutes. Crumble the meat into small pieces and add to the vegetables. Cook until browned and fully cooked, about 5 minutes. Strain, discarding the fat, and return to the stockpot.

Crush the tomatoes by hand and add to the meat mixture. Fill the empty can halfway with water and add to the meat. Add ½ teaspoon of the salt and ¼ teaspoon of the pepper and bring to a boil. Reduce the heat to low and simmer covered but with the lid slightly ajar.

Cook the sauce for at least 3 hours and up to 5 hours, stirring every 30 minutes. If the sauce begins to stick to the bottom, reduce the heat and stir more frequently, adding a few tablespoons of water if necessary. Taste every hour, seasoning with additional salt and pepper as desired. Serve immediately or cover and refrigerate for up to 2 days.

Bring a large pot of water to a boil. Add the pasta and the remaining 2 tablespoons of salt; cook until just al dente, typically 1 to 2 minutes fewer than the package instructions. Drain and divide among serving dishes. Top each with a generous ladle of sauce and drizzle with the *olio nuovo*. Sprinkle with the cheese or pass separately. Serve immediately.

Brasato di Maiale alla Pugliese
(Braised Pork Shoulder, Puglia Style)

James learned to cook this homey Italian dish during a recent visit to Pia's family. The pork requires 2 hours to marinate and another 4 hours to cook, so plan ahead. If you can't find *caciocavallo*, an aged cow's milk cheese from southern Italy, substitute aged provolone.

Serves 8

4 pounds pork shoulder

Kosher or coarse-grain sea salt

1 bottle medium-bodied red Italian table wine such as Sangiovese or Dolcetto

1 small bunch parsley

1 bay leaf

1 tablespoon whole peppercorns

8 to 10 tablespoons olive oil, divided

1 large yellow onion, roughly chopped

1 tablespoon fresh thyme leaves

Freshly cracked pepper

15 scallions with green shoots attached, outermost skin layer removed

Juice of 1 lemon wedge

1 tablespoon red pepper flakes

¼ cup best-quality extra-virgin olive oil, preferably *olio nuovo*

Grated *caciocavallo* cheese for topping (optional)

Trim the pork of any large chunks of fat, leaving the smaller pieces intact. Cut the pork crosswise into 1- to 2-inch pieces. Season on all sides with 1 tablespoon salt and place in a large bowl. Pour enough wine over to cover; add the parsley, bay leaf, and peppercorns. Cover and refrigerate for 2 hours.

Reserve the marinade and remove the pork pieces. Put them on paper towels and pat lightly to remove some of the moisture.

In a large stockpot, heat 4 tablespoons of the oil over medium high heat until almost smoking. Add one-third of the meat and cook until deep golden brown on one side, about 3 to 4 minutes. Turn and cook until golden brown on the other side, another 2 to 3 minutes. Remove to a bowl. Repeat with the remaining batches, adding more oil if needed.

Rinse the stockpot with water and wipe dry with a towel. Heat 2 table-spoons of the oil over medium high heat. Add the onion, thyme leaves, and a pinch of salt and sauté until soft, about 6 to 8 minutes. Add the reserved marinade and bring to a boil. Place the meat and any juices in the pot, stirring to cover with the marinade. Return to a boil, reduce the heat to low, cover, and simmer, stirring the meat every 30 minutes. Cook until it is fall-apart tender, about 4 hours.

Using a ladle, skim off any fat from the surface and discard. Press down on the meat with a wooden spoon or large fork to break it apart until it is almost shredded. Season with the salt and pepper to taste.

Heat a large sauté pan over medium high heat and add 1 tablespoon of the oil. Cook the scallions until tender, about 4 to 5 minutes. Sprinkle with a pinch of sea salt and a squeeze of lemon juice.

To serve, place the meat on a large platter and spoon the sauce over the top. Sprinkle with the red pepper flakes and drizzle with the *olio nuovo*. Top with the cheese. Serve with the scallions alongside.

Spaghetti with Rapini, Tomatoes, Mint, and Hot Pepper

This is one of James's favorite weeknight suppers—it's fast, easy, and delicious. They key, he says, is using the best olive oil you can find for finishing the dish. "With flavors this simple, you've got to invest in good oil." James recommends using Rustichella or DiCecco spaghetti.

Serves 4 to 6 as a main course

- 3 tablespoons extra-virgin olive oil
- 2 cloves garlic, finely chopped
- 1½ cups crushed San Marzano tomatoes (from a drained 28-ounce can)
- 2 tablespoons kosher or coarse-grain sea salt, plus additional, divided
- Freshly cracked pepper, divided
- 2 cups diced rapini, or broccoli rabe
- 1 pound spaghetti
- 1 tablespoon crushed red pepper flakes
- ½ cup mint leaves, finely chopped
- About ⅓ cup best-quality extra-virgin olive oil, preferably *olio nuovo*

In a large sauté pan, heat the olive oil over medium high heat. Add the garlic and sauté until translucent but not browned, 1 to 2 minutes. Add the tomatoes and bring to a boil. Reduce the heat to low and simmer, uncovered, for 30 minutes or until the sauce is slightly thickened. Season with the salt and pepper to taste and turn off the heat.

Bring a large pot of water to a boil. Add 1 tablespoon of the salt and the rapini. Blanch until slightly cooked with stems al dente, about 5 minutes. Drain and add to the tomato sauce.

Refill the pot with water and bring to a boil. Add the pasta and the remaining 2 tablespoons of salt; cook until just al dente, typically 1 to 2 minutes fewer than the package instructions. Meanwhile, rewarm the tomato sauce over medium heat.

Drain the pasta, return to the pot, and add the tomato sauce. Add the red pepper flakes and toss for 1 to 2 minutes over high heat. Remove from the heat, add the mint, and toss to coat. Divide the pasta among serving plates and drizzle with about 2 teaspoons of *olio nuovo*. Sprinkle with the sea salt and pepper to taste. Serve immediately.

WINE
COUNTRY
UNDERGROUND

~

WINE COUNTRY UNDERGROUND

Mystery wines: A selection of New World and Old World pinot noirs

Cheeses: Cowgirl Creamery St. Pat and Pascal Beillevaire bourboule

Frisée salad with goat cheese and garlic panini

Herb-cornmeal-crusted roasted organic baby lamb chops

Truffle-butter scalloped potatoes

Roasted carrots

Minted peas

Dessert: TBD from the wine cellar

~

CHAPTER 2

"Hmmm, what should we take for Scott and Ross?" my husband, Kevin, asks, sifting through the boxes of wine we've bought on this weekend's trip to Sonoma. "I'd hate to take something too inexpensive."

I point out that we're paying for tonight's dinner, so taking one of our higher-end bottles as a host gift is unnecessary.

After much debate, we settle on a syrah from Forth Vineyards, a small winery run by a lovely couple with whom we chatted in the private tasting cellar earlier in the day. Forth makes interesting wines, but at only $22 we're not convinced the bottle is highbrow enough for this crowd. "Who knows, maybe these guys don't know Gerry and Jan so it will be new to them," Kevin says as we get in the car. But I can sense that he's worried.

Into the wine bag I toss some local candied pecans and chutney we picked up earlier in the day, just to be safe.

"Did anyone try B yet?" asks Ryan, a local Sonoma winemaker in his midthirties as he runs his fingers through his scruffy black goatee. "It tastes like bong resin."

The rest of us aren't sure whether that's a compliment or a cut, but now we've got to taste it. We plunk down our glasses and pick up the second from the left, one of six mystery wines in oversized balloon glasses crammed around our dinner plates.

We swirl, inhale, and sip in unison.

"Not really. It smells more like hash than tastes like it," says Nathan, a lanky, balding thirtysomething sporting a perpetual poker face. "And I hope F is the cheapest wine here. It's being slaughtered by the oak."

Nathan knows his wood. He's a professional cooper who learned the craft of wine barrel making from his father. Nathan doesn't talk much, unless you ask him about wine. Get him going and he'll tell you why he thinks one wine is worthy of cellaring, one is passable but will open in a few years, and one has absolutely no redeeming qualities. This knowledge makes him the perfect person to sit next to at a blind wine-tasting dinner—if you're interested in calling him to task, that is.

Once a month, Scott Beattie, a calm, pensive thirty-two-year-old, and Ross Hallett, his wide-eyed, twenty-four-year-old roommate, invite a half-dozen friends, colleagues, and unfamiliar faces to their modest Healdsburg apartment for a blind wine-tasting dinner. It's a simple act of gathering friends for a dinner party . . . only you don't have to be a friend to get an invitation (well, you have to know someone who knows someone, and working in "the industry"—the food and wine industry, that is—doesn't hurt). The catch? Even friends have to pay for the privilege of playing wine critic for the night.

For these two bartenders—Scott works at Cyrus, the crown jewel of the Sonoma restaurant scene, and Ross at Ravenous, a neighborhood wine country bistro and bar—Mondays and Tuesdays (their days off) are all about banishing the cocktail shaker for the corkscrew.

Ross grew up in the tiny logging town of Port Angeles, Washington, and lived a relatively wine-free life. It wasn't until after he graduated from college, at the ripe old age of nineteen, that he started working in the wine industry—first as a buyer, then as a winemaker's apprentice, and most recently as a cellar hand. He's bartending until he can go back to work for a winery, hopefully as an assistant winemaker. But he's also tossing around the idea of bottling his own wine through a custom crush program.

For Scott, bartending isn't a bridge to another career. His obsession with all things shaken and stirred started during his college years at University of California, Berkeley, when he did time behind some of San Francisco's top bars, including Postrio and Azie, to make extra cash. He hit the wine country after graduation, muddling his way through various high-end restaurant bars before landing at Cyrus, where he's become the go-to mixologist (the fancy new word among foodies for bar chef)—dedicated to both reviving lost classics and inventing memorable new cocktails.

"I hate that word, *mixologist*; it sounds so silly and fabricated," he says. "I'm really just a bartender. I happen to really love what I do, mixing up classic cocktails and inventing new ones."

Scott and Ross don't belabor their wine-tasting dinner menus. They don't bother with flowers, candles, or much dusting (although an extra roll of toilet paper is politely set on the bathroom sink). But when it comes to choosing the six feature wines, they'll scour wineries, wine shops, and their own cellar for days, looking for the perfect Grand Cru Burgundy to round out a pinot noir tasting or a heady Napa cabernet to put in the ring against a French Bordeaux.

"Bike, relax, cook, and drink wine—that's what I do on my days off," says Scott. "I try not to think about cocktails. Well, other than I can't stop myself from popping by the restaurant at least once to make sure the barkeep has enough fresh chrysanthemums and poppies. I can't stand the thought of peaked garnishes."

Scott and Ross had been housemates only a couple of months when they started throwing their dinners. "Scott and I get along so well and both enjoy good food and wine, so inviting a variety of industry colleagues over to taste the stalwarts from my collection seemed the appropriate thing to do," says Ross, matter-of-factly. The dewy glow of his Campbell Soup Kid complexion and his warp-speed conversational style are the only hints of his age.

What started as casual wine country dinner parties have turned into formal tasting dinners, with each guest paying a fee to cover the cost of wine and food. Essentially, it's an underground restaurant in the making where most underground restaurateurs started: word-of-mouth invites haven't yet been traded for mass e-mail lists, and friends of friends are still the main attendees. In a town built around the business of food and wine, it's an opportunity for industry colleagues and new faces to gather, a chance for those who fill our glasses to linger over a glass themselves.

Charging for their wine dinners was a natural progression and one that their guests, all wine aficionados, were perfectly happy to oblige. The wines were too expensive for Scott and Ross to justify funding on their

own, especially when many guests weren't exactly friends—or at least not the kind of friends with whom Ross would want to share his 1982 Emidio Pepe Motepulciano d'Abruzzo, to be opened on an upcoming birthday.

"Wines of the Rhone Valley strike a particular synesthetic resonance for me . . . but I have the unfortunate position to have been born in 1982 [not a stellar year for Rhone varietals, hence the Motepulciano], but nonetheless I plan to open this wine, and several others, on my twenty-fifth birthday with special company."

Popping the bottle at tonight's dinner, speckled with industry acquaintances and friends of friends, isn't quite as satisfying. That is, unless everyone has chipped in to recoup the wine's cost, essentially providing the opportunity for the collector to taste something fabulous from his cellar and replace it with another equally valuable bottle.

The price of dinner varies depending on the cost of the wines. Scott and Ross try to keep dinners around $50, inexpensive enough that even their cash-strapped colleagues—restaurant line cooks, winemaking interns, bar backs—can afford to attend, but just enough so they never (gasp) have to resort to subpar wines. With a total of six to eight guests per dinner and access to wholesale wines through work connections and industry friends, not to mention Ross's well-stocked cellar, the $300 they take in at most tastings goes a long way.

Between the two, Ross is the consummate wine guru, although both participate in selecting the wines for each dinner. Tonight, the theme is pinot noir. A dinner guest with access to heady pinots was in charge of the wine. But this morning he called and cancelled. "So we had to pull together some wines at the last minute, which I really prefer not to do. But hopefully we've managed to come up with an intriguing selection."

Last night, when we were sipping Plum Dandy cocktails at Cyrus, Scott mentioned that his apartment has a fantastic view overlooking the Russian River. We're expecting to see something worthy of a Julie Andrews solo. Kevin circled back around the block again, double-checking the address. "Ya, this is it," says Kevin, as we get out of the car.

It's a subdivided condo in the middle of central Healdsburg, not the frolicking hillside with the storybook snaking river we were expecting. In fact, there isn't a drop of water in sight other than the liquid sludge pooling under a pre-1990 red Subaru with a hood crunched like a fistful of gnarled grapevines. Kevin spies a gate behind the has-been car and we slip through, not sure if we'll be greeted by a shotgun barrel or a glass of Chablis.

Scott gives us a wave from the kitchen window. He's traded his suit and tie for shorts, a short-sleeve button down, and flip-flops. A couple of dinner guests are already here, milling around with a glass of wine.

We hand over the Forth.

"Yeah, we know Forth. Thank you very much," says Scott politely, quickly setting the bottle aside. "Ooh, candied pecans! I love candied nuts. Here, try this with the cheese," he says, handing us a glass of 2005 Montee de Tonnerre Chablis Premier Cru a guest brought.

On the tiny kitchen counter a platter of ripe cheeses oozing with stinky goodness is wedged among a jumble of wine bottles.

"We just love our cheesemonger," says Scott, pushing aside a pile of carrots. "We tell her what we're serving and she finds the perfect match, always perfectly ripe. Have you ever seen purple carrots? I'm sure you have in L.A.

But aren't they amazing? Cook them up and the purple color completely disappears."

In keeping with the wine-tasting format, the cheese selection includes both New World and Old World examples. Tonight it's an unctuous St. Pat from Cowgirl Creamery in Petaluma, California, and Pascal Beillevaire's creamy raw milk *bourboule* from Auvergne. I've tasted the St. Pat, a relatively mild, slightly smoky cheese, several times, but never has it been so ripe and full flavored.

"It's almost dirty tasting. Ohhh, I love it," coos Ross as he bites into the *bourboule.*

It is fantastic but absolutely awful with the wine. As an invited guest, I'd never say as much.

"But it's terrible with the wine," quips Nathan.

Ross doesn't seem the slightest bit irritated by Nathan's comment. Blatant—and occasionally brutal—honesty is the expected norm.

"Did you see the plums when you walked in?" asks Scott. Last night I'd asked whether his description of the Plum Dandy wasn't stretching the truth a bit. It's made with mandarin orange blossom vodka, plum

wine, house-made Chinese five-spice honey, lemon juice, peppermint, jasmine, and, according to the menu, "my neighbor's plums hanging over my fence."

"If it's hanging over into my yard, it's fair game as far as I'm concerned," he says. "I think that's the law, anyway. And I really don't take that many."

Ross is chatting about the wine refrigerator he recently purchased and my husband's ears prick up. He's wanted to buy a new one for years. Ross escorts us to the garage to see his shiny new seven-hundred-bottle seven-foot-tall wine refrigerator. No car in sight, but the wine cellar is front and center. It's a real beauty, I must admit.

"No way. Don't even think about it," I tell Kevin. "We hardly have room for the one we've got."

Ross is ignoring our conversation, readjusting a few bottles so the labels are perfectly aligned. He's amassed an impressive collection of more than five hundred wines, with particular emphasis on Italian Barolo—his favorite —from the 1996, 1999, and 2001 vintages. "These are the years, in my experience, that represent classic Barolo structure, perfume, and longevity in the cellar," he explains. "Barolo is a wine of mythical agreeability that develops ethereal perfume and texture at its peak."

We definitely should have brought the more expensive Napa cab.

After Ross and Scott choose the wines for the blind tasting, they develop the menu.

"Scott's really more of the cook between us," says Ross, popping a piece of Gorgonzola into his mouth. Scott has been in the kitchen since we arrived. The highlight of tonight's feast is one of his favorite recipes: roasted organic baby lamb chops in an herbed cornmeal crust with Ross's truffle-butter scalloped potatoes.

Occasionally, Scott will get his hands on prime organic meats at wholesale prices from the restaurant, but usually he has to buy from the specialty store down the street. It cuts into the wine budget, but he feels the quality ingredients are "well worth it."

Scott closes the oven door just as Dawnelise, a sales manager at Iron Horse Vineyards, knocks. She has a 1994 magnum of sparkling Iron Horse Blanc de Blanc tucked under her arm and hands it to Scott. She has a genuine warmth, an addictive glow that fills the room. "Ah, so we got the newlywed out of the house," says Scott, giving her a big hug.

Mikaela, a new pastry assistant at Cyrus who moved to Healdsburg last week for the job, slips in while the door is still open. "Don't I know you?" Dawnelise asks. It turns out Mikaela worked in the Iron Horse tasting room years earlier. And Nathan's mom was the chef at Iron Horse for thirty years. Healdsburg, and all of Sonoma County, is small-town living even with a constant influx of new residents.

Ross pops the Iron Horse. It's a "lost" bottle that was found in the winery cellar three months ago and hadn't been disgorged (the process of removing residual yeast in the neck of a sparkling wine).

"Oh, you know us; we find lost bottles all the time—they pop up when we clean out," Dawnelise says. The winemakers in the room look nonplussed, as if it's just as easy to lose wine as it is car keys.

"Oh shit," Scott mutters, hoping no one else will hear. The panini brushed with garlic and olive oil burned to a crisp while he was tending to the lamb.

"Just cut the burned part off; no one will notice," whispers Dawnelise. A little creative cropping turns the blackened toast into oddly shaped but artfully erratic oversized croutons with a smear of goat cheese. Problem solved.

Dinner is almost ready. The dining room table fills the entire breakfast nook and into the living room opposite a circa-1985 velour sectional sofa and a hodgepodge of hand-me-down bachelor furniture. The glorious view of the Russian River is here, too, right outside the sliding glass door, only it looks a bit more like a reptile-friendly swamp than a scenic wine country river.

The six tasting wines, each wrapped in a brown paper lunch sack and marked with a bold letter in black ink, are lined up in the center of the table. Ross opened and bagged each wine before we arrived and is now dividing them among our tasting glasses. "Technically, I should be the only one here who knows each wine we are having tonight," he says, reaching over my shoulder to pour wine E into my glass. "But even I don't know which wine is in which bag because I shuffled them up before labeling them."

Ross glances at Scott. Anticipation is mounting. "Is dinner about ready, Scott?" he politely asks. "We're all set over here. I'm happy to help if you need anything."

It wasn't until three years ago that Ross's passion for wine really turned into an obsession.

"It was really amazing, just so great," he says, hardly able to contain his excitement. "I was biking one weekend on a quiet road and this car came around the corner and hit me dead-on. It was really bad. I was all smashed up—broken bones, broken nose, the works. I'd broken my nose as a kid, and I could never smell very well. But this time when the doctor reset it, I could suddenly smell. I mean *really* smell. Food, flowers, everything. I took a sip of wine and a click went off in my head, like this whole world opened up with luscious smells and flavors."

Scott places the green salad with goat cheese toasts in front of each guest and takes the empty seat next to me. The rest of us have been swirling our wine, stealing sips without comment, waiting for everyone to get settled.

Normally only five wines are featured, but Ryan brought an unlabeled 1999 Marcassin, a house wine (a blend of unused wine after bottling not meant for resale) he got from his roommate who works at the winery. Plus, we know one of the wines is a 1999 Whitethorn from Hirsch Vineyard on the Sonoma coast. Ross let it slip that the winemaker is back after a seven-year hiatus, so he thought it appropriate that we try one of her predeparture wines. And we also know that all are pinot noir—three New World and three Old World, one of which is a French Grand Cru. Not exactly a completely blind tasting.

"F smells like cardboard and packing tape," says Nathan, starting us off.

"Yeah, but good brown packing tape, not that cheap white stuff that never works," says Ross, the wineglass pressed against his nose.

Packing tape? Maybe I can hang with this crowd. "I wouldn't want to put that in my mouth again," Nathan announces. "Ever."

"I kind of like it; it's intriguing," says Dawnelise. She's the peacemaker tasting type, opinionated but never punchy and always encouraging other tasters to say what they think.

Kevin hasn't said much either, although I know he has an opinion. Not that there is a whole lot to add when you're at a blind tasting with a cooper, a winemaker, and a kid with a cellar full of wine worth more than your car. But fortunately, this is a polite crowd. Opinionated, yes, but no wine jerks.

"We didn't invite one of our friends who can get a little rough with his opinions," confesses Scott. "It's easy to take what he says the wrong way."

Scott and Dawnelise clear the salad plates. "Dinner's ready. I just need to warm up the peas," says Scott, taking a break from the wine debate to finish dinner. The rest of us are too involved in our wine to notice. And besides, we're paying guests, so we don't have to help out in the kitchen, right?

The main course is a good complement for the pinot, although no one seems to care much other than me. Food . . . now that's something I can thoughtfully discuss. Scott carefully slices the chops, checking to see if they're done. They're perfectly medium rare, juicy and tender. He piles three on each plate and Dawnelise follows with a generous scoop of truffle-butter scalloped potatoes, roasted carrots, and minted peas.

"This one is a little odd so it must be the Marcassin house blend," says Ryan.

"It was aged somewhere between 20 percent to 40 percent in French oak, the rest New World oak I'm guessing," says Nathan.

Exactly what I was going to say.

"OK, time to vote," declares Ross, looking at our empty wineglasses. "Which one does everyone think is the Grand Cru?"

At $125, the Grand Cru is the most expensive wine in our tasting, so by default it becomes the premier wine.

Nathan, Ryan, and Kevin agree on A; the rest of us are still undecided. Considering they've been the most consistently correct—or at least consistently vocal—about tonight's wines, I should side with them. But I go out on a limb with D.

Ross disappears and returns with the wine list, one for each guest, complete with the prices (primarily wholesale) paid for each.

∼

A Rene Leclerc, Griotte-Chambertin, Grand Cru, 2005, $125

B Philippe Livera, Gevrey-Chambertin, Clos Village V.V., 2005, $37

C Whitethorn, Hirsch Vineyard, Sonoma Coast, 1999, $40

D Rene Leclerc, Gevrey-Chambertin, Lavaux St. Jacques, 1er Cru, 2005, $60

E Cobb, Coastlands Spivak Vineyard, Sonoma Coast, 2005, $44

F Marcassin, Sonoma Coast Blend, Sonoma Coast (house wine, not available for sale)

∼

The $125 Grand Cru is bottle A. Nathan, Ryan, and Kevin were correct. They all look pleased.

I got every wine wrong. But I'm really more concerned about getting that truffle potato recipe.

Ross appears with a 1998 Thierry Allemand Cornas Chaillot. Ryan was headed for the door but decided to stay. "Wow," says Dawnelise. "Now that's a dessert—heaven in a glass."

But all good things must come to an end, and we've long since hit our saturation point. It's time to thank our hosts, pay the bill (cash only please, no tips), and head back to our hotel. We had arrived as acquaintances, drank some stellar wine, and left as friends.

Is it a full-fledged underground restaurant or a dinner party with a few unexpected guests and a bill at the end of the night? The mass e-mail list and glossy Web site with hundreds of subscribers may be inevitable in the near future, but for now, Scott and Ross don't want to "share our Grand Cru with just anyone."

Tonight, we're perfectly content to be those just anyones.

RECIPES

Minted Peas

Serves 6

1 pound fresh sugar snap peas

Ice water for blanching

3 tablespoons unsalted butter

¼ cup chopped fresh mint

Pinch kosher salt

Pinch freshly ground black pepper

Bring a medium pot of water to a boil and add the peas. Blanch for 1 minute, until just tender. Drain immediately and plunge into a bowl of ice water to halt the cooking. Drain and set aside.

In a medium sauté pan, melt the butter and add the peas. Stir in the mint, salt, and pepper, tasting to adjust seasonings. Serve immediately.

Scott's Herb-Encrusted Rack o' Lamb

Serves 6 to 8

½ cup finely chopped Italian parsley

¼ cup finely chopped mint

2 tablespoons finely chopped tarragon

2 cloves garlic, finely chopped

½ cup panko (Japanese bread crumbs)

1 teaspoon kosher salt

1 teaspoon freshly ground black pepper

1 tablespoon extra-virgin olive oil

2 racks baby lamb (8 ribs each), trimmed of excess fat

Dijon mustard for rubbing as needed

In a small bowl, combine the parsley, mint, tarragon, garlic, panko, salt, and pepper. Add the oil and mix well until thoroughly combined. Set aside and preheat the oven to 400°.

Meanwhile, heat a large sauté pan over high heat. Add 1 rack of lamb, fat side down, and sear until golden brown, about 5 minutes. Set aside and sear the second rack. Place the racks on a roasting rack (or on a grate over a sheet pan) and bake for 15 minutes or until a meat thermometer inserted in the center reaches 125° (for medium rare). Remove the racks and rub the fat side with the mustard.

Divide the panko mixture between the 2 racks and pack down the mixture onto the mustard. You should have a ¼-inch layer of the mixture on each rack. Bake for an additional 3 to 5 minutes for rare and a few minutes longer for medium rare, or until the racks are nicely browned. Cut each rack into 3 to 4 chops and serve.

Ross's Truffle-Butter Scalloped Potatoes

Serves 8

10 medium or 15 small Yukon gold potatoes

1 tablespoon freshly toasted black peppercorns (see Note)

2 teaspoons kosher salt

2 tablespoons extra-virgin olive oil

4 tablespoons (¼ cup) truffle butter, such as TartufLanghe, melted

6 ounces Abbaye de Belloc or aged Emmentaler, finely grated

4 sprigs fresh thyme (leaves only)

1 cup heavy cream, divided

Note: To toast black pepper, sauté in a dry pan over medium heat
until nutty and slightly browned, about 2 minutes.

Preheat the oven to 400°. Leaving the skins on, wash and thinly slice the potatoes into ¼-inch discs.

Grind the peppercorns and salt in a mortar and pestle until coarse; sprinkle on the bottom of a 9- by 13-inch glass baking dish. Add the potatoes, oil, butter, cheese, thyme, and ¼ cup of cream. Toss until thoroughly combined.

Bake for 35 to 45 minutes, drizzling with ¼ cup of cream every 10 minutes until all the cream is used and the potatoes are tender. Remove from the oven and cut into squares. Serve immediately.

CACHÉ

~

CACHÉ

LIPITOR NOT INCLUDED

Caché cocktail

"Pigs in a blanket" with Salumi lamb sausage
and house-made black currant ketchup and Chianti mustard

1st COURSE

Bacon-wrapped bacon

2nd COURSE

Award-winning mac 'n' cheese, Thomas Kemper root beer-braised
short ribs, creamed leeks

3rd COURSE

House-made dulce de leche cheesecake with Valrhona chocolate sauce

suggested donation $50

~

CHAPTER 3

"It's fun to have dinner with strangers, but sometimes, well, you know, it's a lot more fun with friends," explains Tamara, a hairstylist and personal shopper who is hosting tonight's dinner in the backyard of her 1930s home in Columbia City, a revitalized neighborhood in south Seattle. Only she isn't exactly the host. That title officially goes to Caché, a weekly underground restaurant run by Robyn out of her boyfriend Will's Belltown loft.

Robyn, a petite, soft-spoken twenty-four-year-old, doesn't usually take Caché on the road. She's perfectly content cooking in her familiar kitchen where everything is an arm's reach away: pungent spices spilling from the pantry; mixing bowls of every size; a refrigerator full of butter, cream, and fresh herbs. But Tamara is a good friend and loyal Caché customer, so Robyn agreed to cook at her house—just this once.

Tonight's dinner, "French Laundry Night II," is a reprisal of a French Laundry tribute dinner held several months earlier. Tamara was so impressed by the food and Caché camaraderie that she asked Robyn to host a dinner for a group of friends.

Tamara bounds into the kitchen, a supermarket bag held in each arm. "I got the pound cake. And extra chips, just in case," she says, tossing back her foot-long mane of perfectly coiffed brunette curls. The pound cake was

Tamara's idea. Store-bought anything would never make an appearance at a typical Caché dinner.

It's hard not to like Tamara. She's bubbly and engaging, always wearing a perky smile. Her home, a "real fixer-upper," is beautifully restored, from the wood floors and original molding to the toolshed turned party space out back. She did everything herself, including paving the walkway to the backyard.

Robyn is hunched over a tray of foie gras, carefully pulling the veins from each plump, rosy lobe with a paring knife. She glances up and smiles at Tamara, but says nothing.

"Ooh, don't you just love those gurgling chocolate fountains? And who doesn't like a potato chip dipped in chocolate. Right, Robyn?" Tamara laughs and gives her a wink.

At the far end of the kitchen, Will is organizing martini glasses in neat rows. "Have you tried my signature cocktail?" he asks, pulling freshly squeezed pink grapefruit juice from a cooler packed with bar essentials for tonight's dinner.

Will, thirty-four, is Robyn's go-to and only Caché employee: bag boy at the farmers market, prep cook, maître d', bartender, server, and dishwasher. During the week he runs his small architecture firm out of his loft. "I've got to make money designing houses so we can afford to do these dinners!"

Robyn pulls the white-truffle custards out of the oven and gives them a gentle shake. They're perfectly set, barely shimmering. She looks relieved. She doesn't know this oven and is worried the food will not be up to her exacting standards. It doesn't help that tonight's menu was inspired by the French Laundry. Expectations will be high.

Robyn and Will have a soft spot for the French Laundry. They met on eGullet.com, the popular foodie Web blog, chatting about their favorite foods, recipes, and restaurants (with the French Laundry topping the list, although neither had eaten there). A first date wasn't easy to arrange—Robyn lived in Vancouver, British Columbia, Will in Seattle—until one of Robyn's girlfriends scored a reservation for four at the French Laundry.

Robyn hadn't planned to invite Will. The dinner was part of a girls' weekend in Napa, but at the last minute one friend cancelled and they had an extra seat at the table.

"Yeah, she just *had* to invite me!" he recalls.

"Well, really we would have paid a penalty, so I figured why not invite Will," says Robyn. "And besides, it was a safe way to meet him in person, with friends. I mean, we'd met over a blog, so I wasn't going to just fly to Seattle or invite him up to Vancouver or anything like that."

Within a couple of months, Robyn had packed her bags and moved into Will's loft. Dinner must have been really good.

Will pours a few ounces of grapefruit juice into a cocktail shaker, adds a generous splash of gin, and gives it a good shake. He strains carefully, adds two drops of bitters—"homemade, from a neighbor who makes like eight different ones and passes them around to friends"—and pours the concoction into a martini glass.

"I've been trying to brush up on my bartending skills, and I think I've really hit it with this one. See what you think," he says, handing over the Caché Cocktail, now a predinner staple at every event.

It's very good—the tart grapefruit juice balances the floral scent of the gin and herbal bitters.

"Will's cocktails keep guests busy while I'm finishing up dinner and we're waiting for the last people to arrive," Robyn says. "Give them a cocktail and they don't realize forty-five minutes have passed and they haven't sat down yet."

The doorbell rings.

"Tamara, please tell me your friends are not here a whole hour early!" says Robyn, looking visibly flustered for the first time.

It's Kyle, a self-proclaimed wine geek in his midthirties who works at Pike & Western Wine Shop in Pike Place Market downtown. He's carrying a beat-up cardboard box filled with a dozen wine bottles.

"I am so glad you're here tonight," says Will. "You don't know how much I struggle with your wine notes each night, trying to remember what I'm supposed to say."

For Caché dinners, Kyle prepares cue cards with in-depth descriptions of each wine, including why it pairs well with the upcoming dish. "Aw, come on—it's not that hard," he says, blushing as he sets down the wine.

Robyn and Will met Kyle when they brought the menu for their first dinner to the wine shop, hoping for a couple of pointers. Kyle came back with a box of his favorite wines and a stack of index cards for Will.

"We give Kyle our menu, and they just laugh at the shop when we tell them our budget," says Robyn. "But he still manages to come up with great pairings."

Kyle doesn't usually come to Caché dinners, but tonight Robyn needed an extra pair of hands. He lines up the bottles on the counter. "Just wait until you taste this one—it's going to blow you away with the foie gras. Well, I hope. Oh dear, did I forget to bring the decanter?"

Tamara doesn't have one, nor does she have a funnel.

"I'm a cocktail girl, ya know?" she laughs. "How about some Tupperware? Will that work?"

Kyle politely declines the plastic tubs she pulls from the cabinet. He spies a glass carafe in the cabinet that he can use as a decanter. After he's tasted each wine to make sure it's not corked, he pours it back into the bottle using a makeshift funnel from a piece of Robyn's parchment paper.

"We're jerry-rigging the wine! Now the party has really started! Whoohoo!" cries Tamara.

It works—at first—until the parchment paper gets too wet and wine spills over the counter and the floor. Kyle cleans up the mess and gives up on the decanting. "Well, I hate that it won't be properly aerated for your guests."

The doorbell rings again. It's Karl, tonight's volunteer server—only he forgot to tell Robyn and Will he was coming, so Kyle came in his place.

Karl was a guest at Caché's "Anthony Bourdain French Bistro Night," a feast on a par with the "Lipitor Not Included" dinner that followed a few weeks later. Both menus were celebratory indulgences of fat—bacon, foie gras, and duck fat, with plenty of heavy cream in Robyn's mac 'n' cheese to wash it all down. Karl was so taken with the meal—"What's not to like about an all-meat dinner?"—that he volunteered to help. Carrying a few plates in exchange for free food, wine, and good times was too good an offer to refuse. He's been here three weeks in a row, the longest consecutive run for a Caché volunteer assistant.

"Oh yeah, I did get the e-mail asking if I'd be able to help out, but I guess I forgot to reply. C'mon Robyn, you know I don't mesh well with computers on the weekends," he bellows, chuckling. "I figured I'd just show up. That's cool, right?"

The first guests have arrived and are milling around the kitchen. Robyn looks surprised. She didn't hear the doorbell ring.

Robyn is used to Will's 780-square-foot loft where she can keep a watchful eye on the front door from the galley-style kitchen and gauge the crowd while Will greets arriving guests. "I knew it would be different tonight, but I didn't really think that much about it," she says, a little flustered by the number of people congregating in the kitchen. She gives Will a glance and he ushers them outside with promises of his signature cocktail.

What Robyn does think about is food. Growing up in Vancouver, she ate her mom's traditional Cantonese and Shanghai cuisine every night: Hoison sauce, five-spice powder, and preserved vegetables were her family's pantry staples—not a drop of barbecue sauce or squeeze of ketchup in sight. At school Robyn secretly hoarded hot dogs at sporting events, wiped up every last bite of spaghetti with meatballs at girlfriends' dinner tables, and spooned extra salsa on chin-dribbling tacos from the taqueria down the street.

During college and in the two years that followed, Robyn became "obsessed with pastries," as she put it. She posted photos of her creations on eGullet.com—chestnut cake with sultana grapes and rosemary, brioche bread pudding with cinnamon chocolate sauce, matcha cheesecake with almond crust—and local chefs took notice. The pastry chef at Feenie's invited her to intern at the restaurant, and when Rare's chef couldn't afford a pastry chef, he called Robyn for menu ideas. Her suggestion? A Michel Cluizel chocolate ganache tart. She made it for the restaurant's opening night.

But working in a chaotic kitchen wasn't nearly as much fun as experimenting at home for friends. So she ditched the kitchen internship, started a food blog, and worked her way through her favorite cookbooks, cooking each night alongside her favorite culinary impresarios: Thomas Keller, Mario Batali, Suzanne Goin, and Anthony Bourdain.

Then she met Will.

One guest walks through the door and announces she's pregnant. Squeals of excitement all around, except in the kitchen. There isn't a bottle of bubbly water or any other nonalcoholic beverage to be found.

"You mean she doesn't have *anything*, not even in the pantry that we can chill really fast?" Robyn whispers to Will. Karl offers to run to the grocery store and "scare up some Pellegrino."

Bubbly water is an easy problem to solve. Others, like pesky last-minute cancellations, are not. At a twelve-seat dinner, the already slim margin is squeezed even tighter when a guest casually cancels the day of the event (Robyn and Will don't have a formal cancellation policy). With an e-mail list numbering more than five hundred and rarely a diner at the table whom Robyn and Will know, dealing with guests who expect a full-service restaurant can be a problem.

"We sell out within minutes of posting a dinner online," says Robyn. "But people don't seem to understand we're still really tiny, so we can't afford mishaps."

So far, those who cancelled offered to pay for their seat, and Robyn gratefully accepted.

"But the worst was that woman who showed up at our all-pork tasting dinner," says Will.

Robyn rolls her eyes. "This woman walks in and casually says that she doesn't eat pork—at all. I'd been working on the menu for days and didn't have anything in the house other than pork, literally, so I had to send Will to the store," Robyn recalls.

As usual, the menu had been listed on Caché's Web site months in advance. Even the dessert, a Valrhona chocolate ganache tart with chocolate sable crust, sprinkled with bacon brittle and caramelized pecans, featured pig parts.

"It was a *pork* tasting. It's not like I can change the menu at the last minute. I just don't have a stocked restaurant kitchen, but sometimes people come to our house and act like I should," Robyn says. "Mostly, though, the guests have been very courteous."

Robyn has a voracious appetite for fat: fatback, lard, bacon, and oils of every kind. And not just to grease the pan or season a dish. Here, they're the main course. In typical Caché fashion, the menu tonight isn't exactly light: two heavy cream custards, one with truffles, one with foie gras; a generous hunk of foie gras atop pan-fried duck breast; and dessert.

"My favorite thing she makes is the bacon-wrapped bacon," says Will. "It's *really* good."

One lazy afternoon when Robyn was experimenting with pork belly simmered in Asian spices, he suggested she wrap the pieces in bacon, his favorite food.

"That one was definitely Will's idea," says Robyn, grinning. "Even I wouldn't think about wrapping bacon in bacon."

The last of Tamara's friends has arrived, forty-five minutes late. Robyn is up to her elbows in foie gras, and those white-truffle custards are taking up all the counter space. They need to get on the table, pronto.

Tamara's garden is straight out of a magazine centerfold, with cobblestoned steps leading to an adorable wooden shed lit by antique lanterns, a twenty-seat banquet table lined with lime green votive candles and pink-handled cutlery, and strategically placed large-bulb string lights hanging overhead.

I take a seat at the end of the table next to a Brazilian software engineer who recently moved to Seattle for a Microsoft job. Or so I overhear from his discussion with another guest at the opposite end of the table. He's busy ogling his new girlfriend and is completely turned around in his chair with the back of his head in my face.

Fortunately, the woman sitting across from me couldn't be lovelier. "You just *have* to come in for a latte tomorrow and taste our espresso—it's amazing. We pull it by hand. And you should see what my staff can draw in the foam!" Yuki, the manager of a local artisan coffee shop next to Tamara's salon, says.

Tamara leans over and introduces herself to the engineer. Apparently not everyone at the dinner is one of her close friends.

Karl, Will, and Kyle bring out the first course, those white-truffle custards taking up precious counter space. Robyn comes to the table; she's a bit timid (she looks more comfortable in the kitchen than she does with all eyes turned toward her), and she introduces the dish before quietly disappearing back to the kitchen.

Kyle stands front and center and clears his throat to get our attention. He's in his element, waxing lyrical about the nonvintage Foss Maria Prosecco he's chosen to go with the truffle custard. I inhale the fruity Prosecco as he explains why he selected such a dry, crisp style to cut the richness of the heavy cream and accentuate the truffles. It appears that I'm the only one listening.

"It just kind of happened," Robyn explains, searing generous slices of foie gras until they're golden brown. "We had attended Gypsy [another Seattle underground restaurant] in June 2006—it was filmed for Anthony

Bourdain's *No Reservations* television show—and thought we could possibly do something similar but more casual and at a lower price point."

For $50 you can sit tableside at "Throwback to the 50s: bouffants, cocktail dresses, and cigarette holders encouraged," a flashback dinner spiked with twenty-first-century luxuries: deviled egg with fresh truffles; quiche Lorraine with artisan applewood-smoked bacon; pan-roasted oysters with leeks, wild mushrooms in cream sauce, and caramelized shallots; Bananas Foster with homemade pound cake and bourbon-vanilla ice cream. An extra $10 buys a seat at dinners like "All Hail the Duck," with house-made duck prosciutto; duck rillettes on toasted baguette; duck gizzard confit on warm lentils; Toulouse-style cassoulet with duck confit, salumi, pancetta, and pork shoulder. And for dessert? Foie gras tarte tatin.

Even without Will's infamous cocktail and the thoughtful wine pairings, the price of Caché dinners is a bargain for the quality of the food. It's not surprising to hear Robyn say their biggest challenge has been keeping prices low. She spends 50 percent to 60 percent of her budget on ingredients—Grade A Hudson Valley foie gras, eighteen-year-old aged balsamic vinegar, organic meats and produce. A portion goes to wine and incidentals, and whatever is left—assuming no major mishaps or unexpected customer requests—goes in their pocket . . . typically around $100.

"I don't really want to raise the price—the money isn't our first priority," she says. "I look forward to our Sunday dinners each week—I love meeting new people, I love cooking new menus . . . and since our relationship was born out of a mutual love for good food, I think it's only fitting that we've started this venture so we can share it with other people."

Brent, a peppy thirty-two-year-old tattoo-covered devout Christian, arrives in the middle of the first course. He's just driven in from Portland, where he was buying sound equipment for his moonlighting gig as a hip-hop DJ.

"Actually, it's trance music," he politely corrects me. His tight blue knit shirt has tiny tears along the underside of each armpit that look like they might burst at any minute from his bulging biceps.

Brent is Robyn and Will's neighbor and personal trainer. They invited him—and me—to Tamara's party as their guests. "I'm usually at the gym day and night, so this dinner is going to be exciting, no matter what," he says, looking around the table for bread.

He recently hired Robyn as his private chef. "She prepares these killer meals for me—eight hundred calories each, three times a day and 30 percent fat, 40 percent protein, 30 percent carbs—really good stuff."

The custard is fantastic. It's heady with the scent of truffle, simmering under the weight of the black truffle ragout and aged balsamic vinegar-lychee reduction. "This is really rich stuff, don't you think?" says Brent as he takes the tiniest bite. "I mean good and all, but rich. Anyway, have you heard about this new fitness program I developed called Animal Fitness Systems?"

"Another custard?" Brent whispers as Will sets down the next course.

Kyle is standing at the head of the table waiting for his class's undivided attention. By this point, after cocktails and several generous pours of wine, attention spans are short. Brent is telling Yuki where to find the best sushi in Seattle (she grew up in Japan and has lived in Seattle more than twenty years) and the pregnant woman is talking about the store with the cutest maternity clothes (no one else in the crowd is, or has even been, pregnant).

Kyle clinks a glass.

"Yuki, you've *got* to go to Rain Sushi. It's the bomb. And tell them you know me—you'll get a free shot! Seriously!" Brent promises.

The wine is a 2006 Bernhard Frei-Laubersheimer Fels Gewürztraminer Spätlese. Kyle espouses his views on foie gras and classic sweet German wine pairings, like this one from a vineyard "with sloping hills and the perfect amount of sweetness to balance the decadently rich foie gras custard."

My spoon is in the ready position. The foie gras custard is topped with mahogany-colored, roasted Santa Rosa plums and a drizzle of ten-year-old balsamic vinegar. Beneath it is a silky puree of foie gras, Gewürztraminer, and heavy cream. It's even better than the first custard.

Brent notices I've wiped my dish clean and polished off the last sip of wine.

"Hey, do you want mine?" he leans over the table and whispers. "She's a great chef and all, but I'm just not into weird stuff."

"Now we're talking," says Brent as Will brings out the main course, a gigantic half duck breast on a bed of sautéed Swiss chard. Off to the side is an equally generous slice of foie gras with sautéed figs. A main course like this, paired with a good glass of wine, at a posh Seattle restaurant would likely set you back well over the $60 we're paying for tonight's dinner.

Kyle's been talking about the sauce served with the duck since he walked in the door.

"The duck breast and foie gras, no problem, but that sauce—I couldn't sleep last night I was so worried. If I could have chosen the $70 bottle, I know it would have been a home run, but with the $40 bottle—and even that was beyond the budget—I'm worried."

He brought the $70 bottle, just in case.

Robyn throws in a little of this and that when she cooks, whatever flavor strikes her fancy that day. Yesterday, as she was making the sauce, she was drinking root beer, so she poured a touch into the slow-simmering amalgam of beef and duck stock with Madeira, thyme, rosemary, and bay leaves. Voila! Root beer sauce.

The duck and foie gras are excellent. And so is the sauce.

"This dinner probably isn't on my 30-40-30 diet. I'm gonna have to go home and have some protein shakes to even it out," announces Brent.

"Uh, Tamara, can you come here a second? We've got a little problem," says Will.

The chocolate fountain is sputtering large globs of chocolate everywhere.

"Well, I guess we'd better dig into the pound cake, right?" Tamara says, smiling.

Dessert is a lemon cream tart with pine nut crust, crème fraîche, and two-day-old honeycomb. The crust is meltingly tender with a pleasant crunch from the pine nuts, a French Laundry recipe. It's the perfect foil for the tart lemon cream and lightly sweetened crème fraîche.

"Is this real honeycomb?" asks one woman. "Are you *sure* you can really eat the whole thing?"

At this point in the evening, Robyn typically brings out fresh-from-the-oven chocolate chip cookies with a handwritten note asking the guests to leave their "donation" (tips greatly appreciated) on the table. "It's always good to bring out something a little sweet when you're asking for money, don't ya think?"

But tonight we have that overactive chocolate fountain, and Tamara is taking care of corralling the payments since she invited all the guests.

"Wait! Did you try a chip dipped in chocolate? It's really good, I promise— c'mon!" Tamara tries to convince a friend who is headed toward the door.

After their dinners Robyn and Will like to sit with their guests and enjoy a glass of wine. "It's one of my favorite times, just hanging out and chatting with our guests when all the work is done," Robyn says.

After Tamara's friends leave, Robyn and Will join Brent and me at the end of the table. Kyle and Karl pull up chairs. The conversation is—not surprisingly—about food: animal-style burgers at In-N-Out; a killer

deep-fried slow-roasted pork shoulder at a diner in town; what to serve for dessert at Robyn's upcoming "Praise the Lard" dinner.

What's next for Caché? For now Robyn and Will are happily dishing up bacon-wrapped bacon and expanding the palates of personal trainers and foodies in the greater Seattle area.

"Hopefully we can just keep it up; it's pretty expensive," says Robyn. "I don't know what it's going to turn into."

"Well, I think maybe we should change our motto," suggests Will. "Long live lard."

Note: To protect the identity of Caché's organizers, pseudonyms have been used for their names.

RECIPES

Bacon-Wrapped Bacon

Will's favorite dish has become a Caché staple. It takes some time to prepare, but "believe me, it's worth it," says Will. Robyn likes to serve it as a starter with olive oil–drizzled frisée, but you can also pass it as a simple but memorable appetizer. The pork belly and sauce can be prepared up to 24 hours ahead. Wrap the pork belly with bacon and bake just before serving. Count on two per person; it's addictive.

Makes 20 passed appetizers or 10 starters

    3 pounds thick, meaty pork belly, skin on

    1 3-inch knob ginger, peeled and sliced into 4 pieces

    4 scallions, cut into 3-inch pieces

    ½ cup packed brown sugar

    ½ cup Shiaoxing wine (aged Chinese rice wine) or dry sherry

    ¾ cup dark soy sauce

    ¾ cup reduced-sodium soy sauce

    1 heaping tablespoon Sambal Oolek (Indonesian chili paste, available at well-stocked grocery stores and Asian markets)

    1 quart homemade chicken stock or low-sodium canned broth

    4 whole star anise

    1 tablespoon ground cinnamon

⅓ cup Chee Hou sauce (soybean sauce, available
  at Asian markets)

20 strips thin- or regular-cut bacon, not thick cut

20 wooden toothpicks

Slice the pork belly into 1-inch-thick strips, then slice into 20 chunks that are about 1-inch high and 3 inches long.

In a large stockpot over medium high heat, combine the ginger, scallions, brown sugar, wine, both soy sauces, chili paste, stock, star anise, and cinnamon. Add the pork and mix well. If the pork is not covered in liquid, add enough water to cover. Bring to a boil, reduce heat to medium low, and simmer, stirring occasionally until the pork is tender, about 2½ hours. Remove from the heat and cool slightly. Using a slotted spoon, remove the pork, put in a medium bowl, and set aside (or refrigerate for up to 24 hours and bring to room temperature before baking).

When the sauce has cooled completely, skim off the fat that has solidi-fied on top and discard. Strain the sauce through a fine-mesh sieve, pressing on the solids. Discard the solids. Return the sauce to the stock-pot and add the soybean sauce, stirring to dissolve. Cook over medium heat until the sauce has thickened and you have about 1¼ cups of intensely flavored sauce. Set aside (or refrigerate for up to 24 hours and reheat before serving).

Soak the toothpicks in water for at least 15 minutes. Preheat the oven to 325°.

While the sauce is reducing, wrap 1 piece of bacon around each piece of pork and secure with a toothpick. Place the pork skin side up and 1 inch apart on parchment paper or a silicone-lined baking sheet. Bake the pieces for about 30 to 35 minutes or until the bacon is crispy and golden brown. Remove from the oven.

To serve as a passed appetizer, place the bacon on a large platter garnished with frisée; drizzle each piece with 1 teaspoon of sauce. To serve as a plated first course, top 10 serving plates with a small handful of frisée and drizzle lightly with good-quality olive oil, sea salt, and pepper. Place 2 pieces of the bacon to the side of the frisée and drizzle 1 tablespoon of the sauce on top. Serve immediately.

Caché's Award-Winning Mac 'n' Cheese

Robyn didn't eat much mac 'n' cheese growing up—"my house was pretty much Asian food everything"— but it's one of her favorite dishes. What started as a quest to use 20 leftover cheeses from a New Year's party turned into this decadent version with five cheeses and a panko crust ("It's crunchier than bread crumbs, which can get soggy," she says). The recipe won the gold medal at Union Restaurant's annual mac 'n' cheese contest, beating out entries by several top Seattle chefs. "Definitely not diet food, but soooo good," she says.

Serves 8

1 pound campanelle (bell-shaped) pasta

1 tablespoon plus a pinch of salt, divided

9 slices applewood-smoked bacon, such as Niman Ranch, diced

1 sweet white onion such as Vidalia or Walla Walla, diced

3 cloves garlic, peeled and minced

3½ cups (28 ounces) heavy cream

8 ounces aged white cheddar cheese, cubed

8 ounces Gruyère cheese, grated

8 ounces mozzarella cheese, grated

8 ounces Stilton cheese, cubed

5 ounces Parmigiano-Reggiano cheese, grated

2 tablespoons water

2 tablespoons cornstarch

½ cup (8 tablespoons) unsalted butter, divided

CACHÉ

¼ cup all-purpose flour

½ teaspoon freshly ground black pepper

1 teaspoon minced fresh thyme, or ¼ teaspoon dried

1 teaspoon minced fresh marjoram, or ¼ teaspoon dried

1 teaspoon red pepper flakes

½ teaspoon cayenne

1 ½ cups panko (Japanese bread crumbs)

1 tablespoon chives, finely minced

Bring a large pot of water to a boil. Add 1 tablespoon of the salt. Cook the pasta for 8 minutes. Drain and shock under cold water. Set aside.

In a medium skillet, cook the bacon over medium high heat until the fat has rendered. Add the onion and garlic. Cook until the bacon is crisp and the onions are browned, about 5 minutes.

In a large stockpot, combine the cream, all the cheeses, and the bacon mixture over medium low heat. Cook, stirring constantly, until the cheeses are melted.

In a small bowl, combine the water with the cornstarch. Stir until the cornstarch is dissolved; add to the cheese sauce. Heat until the sauce bubbles gently and is thickened, stirring constantly.

Meanwhile, in a small saucepan over medium high heat, combine 5 tablespoons of the butter and the flour; cook until browned and the mixture smells nutty, about 5 minutes. Add to the cheese sauce with the black pepper, thyme, marjoram, red pepper flakes, and cayenne. Heat until the sauce begins to thicken, about 5 minutes. Add the pasta and set aside, keeping warm.

In a large pan, combine the panko and the remaining 3 tablespoons of butter. Toss until the butter melts and the panko is golden brown, 3 to 4 minutes. Season with a pinch of salt and pepper.

Spoon the warm mac 'n' cheese into 8 serving bowls, then sprinkle with the panko mixture and a pinch of chives. Serve immediately.

——•——

Black Mission Fig Frangipane Tart with Buttermilk Ice Cream

This is one of Robyn's favorite lard-free desserts. "When figs are in season, I just have to turn them into pastries," she says. This recipe makes two 9-inch tarts and serves 16. If you don't need two tarts, halve the recipe or make both tart shells and freeze one unbaked but pressed into the tart pan, for later.

Serves 16

Crust

1 cup (16 tablespoons) unsalted butter, softened

2 teaspoons vanilla extract

¼ cup sugar

2 egg yolks

2½ cups cake or pastry flour

½ teaspoon kosher salt

Beat the butter, vanilla, and sugar until creamy and light in color, about 6 minutes. Add the egg yolks, beating until combined. Stir in the flour and salt until thoroughly combined.

Preheat the oven to 350°.

Divide the dough in half. Wrap each half in plastic wrap and allow to rest in the refrigerator for 1 hour. On a well-floured surface, roll the first half into a 12-inch round and carefully transfer to a 9-inch tart pan. Trim with a knife to form a uniform 1-inch tart edge. Place a piece of parchment paper trimmed to fit the tart pan in the center and fill with pie weights or dried beans. Repeat with the second half.

Bake until the crust is set and beginning to brown, about 20 to 25 minutes. Remove the parchment paper and pie weights and bake an additional 5 minutes or until the crust is golden brown.

Frangipane

4 sticks (2 cups) butter, softened

4 tablespoons all-purpose flour

1 cup sugar

2 cups almonds, finely ground

2 whole eggs

2 tablespoons dark rum

1 tablespoon vanilla extract

24 to 30 fresh Black Mission figs (depending on size), sliced in half

Buttermilk Ice Cream (recipe follows)

In a food processor, pulse together the butter, flour, sugar, and almond meal until smooth. Stir in the eggs and rum. Divide the mixture into the 2 tart crusts, spreading evenly. Arrange half the figs, cut side down, in concentric circles in 1 tart, pushing gently so the figs are partially covered by the mixture but the tops are still visible. Repeat with the second tart.

Bake until the mixture is golden brown and set, 35 to 40 minutes. Cool. Slice into 8 wedges and serve with a scoop of ice cream.

Buttermilk Ice Cream

2 cups heavy cream

1 vanilla bean

6 egg yolks

¾ cup sugar

2 cups whole-milk buttermilk

In a medium saucepan, heat the cream over medium heat. Slice the vanilla bean lengthwise and scrape the seeds into the saucepan. Add the vanilla bean and bring to a simmer. Immediately remove from the heat. Cover and steep for 10 minutes. Discard the vanilla bean.

In a medium bowl, whisk the egg yolks and sugar. Add ¼ cup of the hot cream, whisking constantly. Be careful not to add the cream too quickly or the yolks will curdle. Gradually add more cream, ½ cup at a time, until fully incorporated. Stir in the buttermilk, cover, and refrigerate at least 6 hours but preferably overnight.

Churn in an ice cream maker according to the manufacturer's instructions. Serve immediately or freeze in a tightly covered container for up to 3 days. If frozen solid, let soften on the counter for 20 minutes before serving.

WHISK &
LADLE

In the far reaches of Manhattan's Inwood neighborhood, one woman (with the help of her sister and a boyfriend-ish character) founded a supper club that seemed to stand up against the onslaught of the "bar-restaurant" culture. Abiding by the traditional structure of the dinner party—a cocktail hour, soup course, entrée, then salad—and out of the deeply entrenched belief that all things civilized and debaucherous find common ground on a dining room table, the Whisk & Ladle Supperclub was born.

Now there are three of us, and a 95-year-old factory building on the Williamsburg waterfront is our home. With a reverence for classic cuisines and an overwhelming enthusiasm to create new staple dishes, we present to you the hallowed dinner party. May five-courses and cocktails live on!

—Whisk & Ladle

CHAPTER 4

And now there are four: Norah, a lawyer by day and the resident Julia Child come suppertime; Mark, a math professor and the organizer of the bunch; Danielle, a waitress turned tutor who loves playing hostess; and Nick, a Manhattan bartender who gets his kicks turning out experimental cocktails at home.

What started as a small supper club in Norah's Manhattan apartment has morphed into a twice-monthly underground restaurant run by these four twentysomethings out of their funky Brooklyn loft. Only don't call it a restaurant. And please don't use the word *hipster*.

"We really don't want to be referred to as hipsters . . . and we don't consider W&L a club with members . . . and we prefer not to feel like we're in a restaurant . . . and we have a real aversion to the term *foodie*—what member of the species isn't a foodie, a person who enjoys food? We invite people of all ages, and strive to do so (the oldest guest was seventy-six, the youngest, seventeen) . . . which keeps a certain hipster demographic from developing . . . and we make sure not to book too many people from one party, one profession, or one part of town," explains Mark.

Nick started shaking cocktails for tonight's dinner guests at 8:00 sharp, and my friend Paul, a photographer, and I are running late. I printed the directions from the confirmation e-mail the night before—and naturally left it on Paul's kitchen counter. A train ride back to his loft on the opposite end of Brooklyn was advisable as underground restaurants aren't exactly easy to look up in the phone book.

Paul hasn't been to Williamsburg since the mid-1990s when several of his friends, all struggling artists, lived and worked in the industrial warehouse lofts along the waterfront. These days most of the artists have been replaced by young professionals and grunge hipsters—er, Gen Yers—sipping the cocktail du jour at the trendy neighborhood restaurants and bars.

Paul spots the building. The door is wide open so we walk in, a bit reluctantly. Shouldn't we ring a buzzer? In the hallway is a plain white piece of printer paper with a crudely drawn whisk and an arrow pointing to the left.

"Is this some kind of scavenger hunt? This is going to be fun!" says Paul as we turn the corner to find another clue, only this time the drawing is a ladle.

When I invited Paul as my dinner companion, he had never heard of Whisk & Ladle, although he was well schooled in the underground

restaurant scene in Manhattan. Many of them sounded exclusive—secret entry passwords, $100 price tags—not the underground scene he had in mind. But dinner in a Brooklyn loft for 40 bucks? Now that had real potential for spirited debauchery.

Mike and his cohorts would be pleased to hear that Paul was intrigued—for what they consider the right reasons. Shortly after an article on Gawker, the Manhattan gossip and news Web site, drew attention to Whisk & Ladle in the fall of 2006, the Web site was inundated with droves of e-mails from New Yorkers eager to dine at the "restaurant."

"Anything that says 'dinner reservation for two' in the header I automatically delete without opening," says Mark.

So how exactly do you get in? With only two to three dinners each month and twenty to twenty-five guests at each dinner, it's not easy. Your best bet is to send a wildly creative e-mail (and don't forget to add a catchy header). If you can't get into a regular dinner, perhaps you can swing a spot at one of their one-hundred-person soirées, held every couple of months. Or if you've got a racket and a shuttlecock in your closet, you might want to inquire about membership in their newest club, the East River Badminton Club. The launch party, held in their loft, included live badminton matches—but of course.

Jay Gatsby would be proud.

Another paper sign—this one has both the whisk and the ladle—is on the door at the end of the hallway. Paul knocks but no answer, so we walk in.

"Come in, come in, and put your jackets and purses on the rack," says a voice hidden behind a young woman dangling on an ivy-covered swing, neon-orange cocktail in hand. The coat rack is stuffed with what looks like a lot more than two dozen summer purses and light jackets.

A petite brunette with a wide smile pops out from behind the swing. "Norah," she says, wiping her hands on her apron. We introduce ourselves and she slides back behind the kitchen counter to tend to a large pot on the stove. We're left to make ourselves at home.

At underground dinners this size, a list of "registered" guests is often whipped out, scanned, and checked off. It's a glaring reminder that you're a paying customer, not an invited guest. But here, no such list appears. Nor, for that matter, does anyone give us any instructions. The assumption is that if you're here, you'll know to wander over to the bar, help yourself to the appetizers, and grab a seat on the velour sofa—just like a good friend who's been here a half-dozen times.

The lounge area in the back of the loft is packed, nary a seventy-six-year-old in sight. It's mainly a crowd of early- to late-twentysomethings wearing grunge T-shirts and miniskirts, peppered with a few thirtysomethings in pressed jeans and one, maybe two, parental types wearing penny loafers. And although I have no doubt there have been septuagenarians at a past Whisk and Ladle dinner, tonight Paul and I are doing our part to prevent that dreaded hipster demographic.

"What will it be?" asks Nick as he hands us this evening's cocktail menu. He's decked out in a black button-down shirt and shiny red silk tie—a touch smarmy Vegas dealer, but he manages to pull it off with his soft face and cheery grin.

Before Nick moved into the loft, Norah, Mark, and Danielle always hired a friend to tend bar. Having a professional to set the proper party tone and shake up stellar drinks has always been important to them. Now that they have Nick on board, they can pour the cash they used to spend on a bartender into top-quality ingredients.

And for Nick, known as a bit of a perfectionist when it comes to cocktails, such ingredients are essential. At his day job, he doesn't get to do much experimenting. If the customer wants a gin and tonic, a gin and tonic it is. But at Whisk & Ladle dinners, he can serve whatever he pleases.

I order the blood orange margarita, one of four choices scribbled on the handwritten menu. It's deliciously tart with a hint of sweetness from the orange liqueur. Paul gets the Colombian vodka, a spicy combination of *mate de coca* (herbal tea made from cocoa, coconut, and spices), vodka, and honey.

"Pretty good, actually, but kind of odd," Paul says as he hands it to me for a taste. "Didn't you say he did a peanut-infused vodka cocktail one

time? That sounds interesting." He orders the Friend of a Friend, whiskey and sweetened apple juice with a savory onion garnish.

We like the margarita best. But we couldn't bring ourselves to criticize the bartender-host in his own home, so when Nick asks which cocktail we prefer, we answer with a resounding "They're all excellent!" Not that Nick would bat an eye if we didn't care for one of his creations. In fact, I suspect he wants a genuine answer. It helps him develop even better drinks. And at Whisk & Ladle, sampling flavor combinations you've never tried is part of the fun, and the point. It's a rare treat in a city where tasting something new—and running the risk of not liking it—can be a costly proposition.

Danielle sets a tray of sliced tenderloin and cubed honeydew on the bar. "No, it's not beef, it's kangaroo," she says with a smile. "And did you try the chocolate tart with grapefruit mascarpone over there? Hurry, there aren't many left."

The chocolate appetizer is as bizarre as it sounds. It tastes like a bar of unsweetened baking chocolate topped with bitter grapefruit peel. It's

intriguing but definitely not on my short list of must-have afternoon snacks.

We make our way to the platter of kangaroo. It's been ravaged by the guests and only a few pieces are left. The tenderloin, seared medium rare and thinly sliced, is topped with a kiwi *sambal* (spicy Malaysian relish) dipping sauce.

"This is good, really good," says Paul. "But I'm not sure I'm happy to be gnawing on a 'roo. Gotta think about that."

There's something refreshing about being in such a whimsical, experimental kitchen. You never know what you're going to be served, but you can count on it being unusual. Participating in the kitchen's triumphs and failures is part of the appeal. In the company of such unbridled culinary enthusiasm, such genuine desire to explore new foods and cooking techniques, it's hard not to feel like a proud parent encouraging these young cooks to try, try, and try again. Well, at least as long as it costs around $40 for cocktails (four, no less), a multicourse dinner with wine pairings, and hours of entertainment. In a city where valet parking at Le Cirque is $35 (plus tip), it's hard to nitpick over the occasional odd cocktail and an experimental appetizer gone awry.

Dinner is served Saturday at 8 PM. We send out a confirmation e-mail to our reservation list, and a reminder to our mailing list seven days before. On Monday, roommates with opposite schedules chatter through a flurry of e-mails. Whisk & Ladle does not adhere to any theme or culinary tradition;

we unify the menu items only after we've narrowed down what the best dishes will be. Dishes are established by what we want to cook. Norah wants to make beets, watercress salad, a soup with fish. Mark wants swordfish and avocado flan. The swordfish becomes sea bass, the watercress stays, Danielle adds some homemade ice cream, and Norah decides to light a cake on fire and set it next to the ice cream. A chaotic method of menu selection if not for the fact that each of us wants to make 5 different things every week. Something in the combinations has to work. A theme develops.

—Whisk & Ladle

Mark climbs a ladder in the middle of the loft that leads to a hammock hanging from the ceiling. "Dinner is ready, find a seat," he announces.

Earlier in the evening I counted twenty-two place settings at the dining tables, but there are at least thirty-five people, maybe more, milling around the bar. Maybe this is a first-to-sit, first-to-eat kind of thing.

"We always keep space for friends who confirm as late as the afternoon of the dinner," explains Mark. "This ensures that we have people in our apartment who've been [here] before . . . we prefer not to feel like we're in a restaurant so we encourage friends and former guests to stop by after cocktail hour, when guests are seated, to experience the dinners without being part of the dining room crowd."

Translation—while paid guests are eating (and also before and after dinner), their friends hang out at the bar. Brilliant. A cocktail party for their friends funded by the paid guests.

Norah, the cook of the group, grew up in Westchester County. Her family held large dinners during the holidays, but she says her real inspiration came from her grandmother's formal, multicourse dinner parties. She's always been keen on reviving the parties of days past, when a salad came after the main course and two forks were standard at each place setting.

"My friends just weren't into that kind of thing," she says.

So Norah began hosting small formal dinner parties in her apartment. At first she added a touch of flair to cherished family recipes, lightening holiday sweet potatoes with egg whites and adding a pinch of hot pepper to shortbread cookies. As her culinary confidence grew—no doubt her grandmother wouldn't have added strawberries to the garlic mashed potatoes—so did the number of guests at her dinner parties. A new apartment and a couple of roommates later, and Whisk & Ladle was born.

For the rest of the group, learning to cook has been part of the appeal of hosting parties. "We're learning as we go," says Danielle. "Norah is such a great cook, and I love watching her in action. And to be able to go to the market and know you can spend $300 and not worry about the money, just buy whatever you want. It's so great."

They're a bit like teenagers out with a parent's credit card, only they're buying exotic game and aged tequilas instead of designer T-shirts. It's a lot more fun to experiment in the kitchen with coriander-crusted crocodile tail and prawn meatballs with lingonberry mousse when you're not footing the bill.

My table is filled with the older guests, if you can call a group in their early to midthirties "older." We've migrated to one another, as inevitably happens at many dinner parties, no matter how hard our hosts may have tried to diversify the guest list.

The "dining room" is more flea market funky than downtown chic, with votive candles, candelabras, and Mom's old cotton-weave placemats. It's a hodgepodge assortment with a large wooden table—the breakfast table, judging by the matching chairs—a patio table covered in a floral table-cloth, and a pink Formica table with gold metal legs. Normally, this area of the loft serves as the living room, but the tables are pulled in on a Friday afternoon and the space is transformed into the dining room.

"It is a very livable space when we're not serving dinner," says Mark. "Quite scholarly."

"Did you see the bunnies?" Paul whispers as he pulls out a tiny wrought iron patio chair at the end of our table and wedges himself into the seat.

An enormous chandelier made from a dozen metal rabbits hangs from the ceiling. Norah's welding instructor, Aurora Robson, made it when she lived here.

"Aurora was a pioneer of sorts along with the rest of the early settlers," explains Norah, referring to the building's first tenants, who built the loft

when the building was still a deserted warehouse. At one point Aurora and the other residents were locked out by the housing department for "all manner of housing violations," Norah continues. "I eventually moved into the loft, took over the lease, and was bequeathed the bunnies."

A recently married husband and wife in their late twenties sitting on our right introduce themselves. "I'm actually from New York, unlike most people in Manhattan these days—grew up in Queens. But I'm into real estate these days," he says, scanning the loft. "There aren't a lot of development opportunities left around here, but I'm gonna find them. You've got to come to more remote places like this."

His wife, a friendly blonde from Los Angeles, works at Christie's art auction house in Manhattan. Across from us are a young banker and his girlfriend, a thirtysomething travel director at a publishing company. "Uptown isn't hip like down here, but it's clean," she says. "I know it's not cool, but secretly I really do love living on Park Avenue."

Danielle pours each of us a glass of wine and disappears to the next table.

"What is it, a sauvignon blanc?" Paul asks.

We're told the local wineshop down the street puts together the wine pairings based on each menu, only we don't have a clue what we're drinking. There isn't quite the fanfare made about wine at Whisk & Ladle dinners as there is for the cocktails, although our hosts could have slapped a carafe of house wine on the table and we'd be happy.

"What's this red stuff in the soup?" asks the real estate developer. "It's really different."

We pull out our printed menus: chilled avocado soup with beet puree. I think it's quite good. The developer's wife says he's not a particularly adventuresome eater. "So how'd you guys hear about this place?" asks the developer, swirling his spoon around the edges of the bowl to avoid the beet puree.

"A friend," says the travel manager. "She raved about it so we had to come check it out."

"We read about it on Gawker and it sounded pretty cool. We get tired of the same old thing, eating in the same places, ya know?" he says.

"We could never do this in our apartment because we don't have the room," adds his wife. "We can hardly have four people over to dinner. The only time I go to dinner parties anymore is back in L.A."

Nick turns the music up a couple of notches. Norah and Danielle are dancing around the kitchen, twirling around Mark as he tops each plate of pea risotto with a generous hunk of pan-seared salmon. Danielle stops by to refill our wineglasses, this time a rosé, and asks if we're all having a good time.

"How can you not?" says the developer. "This is such a cool idea. You get to do this every weekend?"

"Pretty much," says Danielle.

Mark and Nick set heaping platters of the risotto and salmon in front of us and clear the soup from the rest of the tables. We've hardly noticed what's been happening at the other two tables—it's easy to forget anyone else is here—but it appears we're a few bites ahead.

"The salmon is really good, but don't you think the risotto has a little too much lemon?" Paul whispers across the table. It's more an observation than a blatant criticism. We all agree—the salmon is tasty, but the risotto could use a little tweaking. There's so much food and wine, however—not to mention the cocktails and pleasant company—that we can't complain. Besides, we'd all like to be invited back.

"Oh no, she's not *that* kind of girlfriend," says the banker when I ask how long he and the travel director have been together. "We're just good friends. What's the next course, anyhow?"

Funny, for a group of people who didn't care much for the risotto, we've all managed to clean our plates.

Norah is slicing the half-dozen miniloaves of bread she just pulled out of the oven. "Portuguese sweet bread," she announces.

Mark comes around with a basket of the steaming slices. Our plates have been cleared, so we balance a piece on our forks. It's a good homestyle 1950s quick bread with a touch of sweetness, something Norah's grandmother might have made.

Danielle pours a big, jammy red. It seems like an odd choice for the next course—a light summer salad with mixed greens and a berry vinaigrette.

"Oh, you don't have to drink it all," she says as I quickly polish off my rosé. "Just throw it in your water glass. We got one course ahead on the wine pairings—the red was supposed to go with the salmon. Oops!"

We've managed to plow through dinner in an hour, less time than we spent sipping cocktails. But there's still more to come—a glass of port served in coffee mugs (by this point they're the only clean receptacles left), and tres leches cake with coconut ice cream for dessert.

"This is excellent," announces Paul, scooping up the last bite of the spongy cake and creamy ice cream. It's the best dish of the night.

"You guys want to go out?" asks the real estate developer. "Are we supposed to pay now, or what? Has anyone been to one of these things before?"

It's the underground dining world's most awkward moment . . . the little matter of the bill.

"Please stay," says Mark as he slips payment envelopes next to each plate. "We've got some friends coming over so you can hang out as long as you want. And you should check out the view from the roof. You can smoke up there, too."

A handmade card is inside each envelope—mine is a grainy color photo of Elvis eating a peanut butter sandwich with the scribbled inscription "Elvis would have eaten you—you're that delicious. $40 . . . XOXO, W&L."

"Are we supposed to leave tips?" asks the developer. It's what separates an underground dinner from a supper club gathering—tips are almost always appreciated . . . and expected.

Nick heads back to the bar as their friends arrive for the postdinner cocktail party. Mark, Norah, and Danielle are scrubbing plates, dancing around the island to Frank Sinatra. Some guests have gone to the rooftop;

others are hanging out at the bar. They're not likely to get a seat at this restaurant again anytime soon.

Norah's grandmother would surely approve. It's exactly how she would have thrown a dinner party. Except for the kangaroo. And that little matter of the bill.

RECIPES

The Freshman Girl

This is one of Nick's most requested cocktails. He infuses the tequila twice to extract the maximum strawberry flavor. Plan ahead; the tequila must be infused for 12 hours.

Makes 1 cocktail

2 ounces Strawberry-infused Tequila (recipe follows)

1 ounce Frangelico

2 ounces freshly squeezed blood orange juice

Ice

1 strawberry

Combine the tequila, Frangelico, and orange juice in a cocktail glass. Stir well to combine and fill the glass with the ice. Garnish with a strawberry.

Strawberry-infused Tequila

1 750-ml bottle good-quality tequila blanco

2 pints strawberries, washed and sliced

Place half the strawberries in a medium bowl and cover with the tequila, saving the bottle. Cover with plastic wrap and macerate for 6 hours. Strain into a clean bowl, pressing on the strawberries to release the juices.

Add the remaining strawberries to the bowl, cover, and macerate for another 6 hours. Strain into a pitcher, pressing on the strawberries to release the juices. Using a funnel, pour the tequila back into the bottle. Strawberry tequila may be stored in the refrigerator for up to 2 weeks.

Date-Stuffed Hanger Steak

Mark loves this dish for a dinner party because it's "a little compli-cated, messy, and really good." Start with Nick's Freshman Girl cocktail and serve the steak with simple roasted potatoes, green salad, and crusty bread.

Serves 4 to 6

8 fresh dates

¾ to 1 pound hanger steak, 3 inches thick, 6 to 8 inches long (ask your butcher to cut it in a single piece)

1 teaspoon ground cinnamon

1 teaspoon powdered turmeric

1 teaspoon paprika

1 teaspoon black pepper

4 cloves garlic, minced

1 1-inch piece ginger, peeled and minced

4 tablespoons maple syrup, divided

2 tablespoons butter

1 teaspoon kosher salt

Cut the dates in half lengthwise and remove the pit. Set aside.

Insert a metal skewer into one end of the meat and force it through the length of the meat. Remove the skewer. Using a knife, make a hole at one end of the meat big enough to fit a knife-sharpening steel (blunt end). Force the steel through the meat to create a large hole. Alterna-tively, use a paring knife to make a small hole at one end of the meat.

With your fingers push half a date into the hole. Use the steel to push it to the center of the meat. Repeat until all the dates are used and are evenly distributed throughout the meat. (If all else fails, slice the meat in half lengthwise, place the dates in the middle, and tie the meat together with two pieces of kitchen twine.)

In a small bowl, combine the cinnamon, turmeric, paprika, pepper, garlic, and ginger. Wearing rubber kitchen gloves (turmeric will stain your hands), rub the meat with the spice mixture. Place the meat in a resealable plastic bag and add 3 tablespoons of the maple syrup. Seal and refrigerate for 6 hours.

Preheat the oven to 400°.

Heat a large, heavy-bottomed skillet over medium high heat until hot, about 2 minutes. Melt the butter in the skillet and add the meat. Sear until golden, about 2 minutes. Flip and repeat. Remove from the heat and place in a roasting pan. Drizzle the meat with the pan juices and any remaining melted butter. Sprinkle both sides with the salt and drizzle with the remaining 1 tablespoon of maple syrup. Roast about 5 minutes for rare, 8 minutes for medium rare. Remove from the oven and let sit for 5 minutes before slicing.

Norah's Sweet Potatoes

Norah adds egg whites to classic whipped sweet potatoes for a lighter consistency. If you are concerned about raw egg whites and salmonella, substitute a pasteurized egg white product.

Serves 6 to 8

> 2 pounds sweet potatoes, peeled and cubed
>
> 5 egg whites
>
> 1¼ teaspoons kosher salt, divided
>
> White pepper
>
> 1 tablespoon butter
>
> 1 tablespoon heavy cream
>
> Zest and juice of 1 grapefruit, separated

In a medium stockpot, bring several quarts of water to a boil. Add 1 teaspoon of salt and the potatoes and boil until tender, 5 to 8 minutes depending on size. Remove the pot from the stove; drain and return the potatoes to the pot.

In a medium bowl or stand mixer, beat the egg whites with a pinch of salt and pepper to stiff peaks. Set aside.

Add the butter, cream, and 3 tablespoons of grapefruit juice to the potatoes and mash with a hand masher until only small lumps remain. Return potatoes to the stovetop over medium low heat. Slowly fold in the egg whites until incorporated. Add ¼ teaspoon salt, pepper, and ¼ teaspoon zest, stirring constantly so potatoes do not burn. Taste, adding more salt and pepper or zest as needed. Serve immediately.

Caramelized Plum Salad with Stuffed Tomatoes and Golden Raisin Dressing

A Whisk & Ladle summer favorite. The caramelized plums are a sweet contrast to the savory goat cheese–stuffed tomatoes and tangy dressing. Choose ripe but not overly soft plums.

Serves 6

1 bunch arugula or dandelion greens, washed, dried, and torn into small pieces

2 cups mixed baby greens

2 tablespoons butter

4 plums, quartered and sliced into ¼-inch wedges

2 ounces dry white wine

Kosher salt and freshly cracked pepper, divided

1 teaspoon ground coriander seeds

2 ounces fresh goat cheese

Zest of ¼ lemon

10 to 12 grape tomatoes, halved lengthwise and seeded

Golden Raisin Dressing (recipe follows)

¼ cup hazelnuts or pecans, finely crushed

In a large bowl, mix the arugula with the baby greens. Set aside.

In a large saucepan, heat the butter until melted. Add the plums and sauté for 1 minute. Add the wine and cook until the plums are soft but not falling apart, about 2 minutes. Season with the salt and pepper to taste. Transfer to a small bowl.

In a small sauté pan, toast the coriander seeds over medium high heat until they smell nutty, about 1 minute. Grind in a coffee grinder and set aside.

In a small bowl, combine the cheese, coriander, zest, and a pinch of pepper. Stir well. Stuff each tomato half with about ½ teaspoon of the mixture. Set aside.

Spoon the dressing over the greens and mix with your fingers. Sprinkle the nuts over the greens and divide among salad plates. Top each plate with the plums and 2 to 3 stuffed tomatoes. Sprinkle with the salt and pepper. Serve immediately.

Golden Raisin Dressing

½ cup golden raisins

½ cup olive oil

3 teaspoons fresh thyme leaves

¼ teaspoon kosher salt

1 teaspoon freshly ground pepper

¼ teaspoon brown sugar

Juice of 1 medium lemon

¼ cup freshly squeezed orange juice

In a small saucepan, boil the raisins with enough water to cover (about 1 cup) until hydrated, about 2 minutes. Drain and return to the saucepan.

Add the oil, thyme, salt, and pepper and simmer for 10 minutes. Set aside to cool. When cooled, add the brown sugar, lemon juice, and orange juice. Transfer the mixture to a blender or food processor and blend until it becomes a paste. The dressing will be thick; thin with a few tablespoons of olive oil if needed, and season with additional salt and pepper to taste.

HUSH

~

CONFIRMATION: Supper Club @ HUSH

WHEN: Thursday, April 19 at 7:30 sharp

WHERE: * * * * * * * * * *

COST: $40 per person

SUGGESTED WINES: Gewürztraminer, Pinot Noir, Merlot, and Pinot Gris

Please feel free to contact us if you have any further questions or concerns.

~ HUSH ~ D.C.'s Supper Club

Thank you for expressing an interest in dining at HUSH. Below is the list of final confirmations. You will find your name and last initial along with a parenthesis indicating the number in your party. At your earliest convenience, please provide us with the name of your guest. Finally, because of our limited space and budget we ask that all cancellations be at least 72 hours prior to the dinner.

Best,
The HUSH Team

~

CHAPTER 5

"I read encyclopedias for fun, you know, after work," announces Robert, a twenty-eight-year-old information technology specialist sitting to my right, in between bites of sweet pea *panna cotta*. "No really, I mean it. What do you do?"

I'm beginning to understand why Anne Horstmann, twenty-six, raised an eyebrow when I switched seats with my cousin, Brent, to give him a little more legroom. My place card was originally next to Anne's sister, Helen, a start-up Web site owner from Philadelphia, and her husband, Steven, an acupuncturist.

Anne is the founder and head chef of HUSH, a small underground supper club in Washington, D.C. Anne hosts intimate six- to seven-course dinners once a month in the apartment she shares with four roommates near Eastern Market. A recent culinary school graduate, she is a line cook under James Beard-award-winning Chef de Cuisine R. J. Cooper at Vidalia Restaurant near Union Station, where working the line means doing whatever is needed, whenever it's needed, and exactly as the chef orders. But once a month, Anne gets to play head chef for a day, leisurely planning a menu around ingredients that inspire her, cooking them however she pleases, and serving them to a group of sixteen guests in her living room.

"It's really more a chance for me to try out new dishes and see what people think of them," says Anne. "And Sid and I both love to entertain until summer, when it's too hot in here to have people over."

My correspondence with HUSH was limited to three e-mails: a confirmation that my reservation request for two was accommodated; a request for my guest's first name; and a basic informational e-mail with the location, time, wine suggestions, and FAQs. And with no Web site, Brent and I have no idea what to expect. It's all refreshingly underground.

Brent and I are driving in from Baltimore. We're concerned about finding parking on a Thursday night—and finding the house. With no phone number to call, we're on our own.

After three circles around the neighborhood, we manage to find the house, a charming three-story Victorian, and score a prime parking spot across the street. We knock on the door but no answer. I peek through the window. It looks like the right place; either that or whoever lives here has decided to fill the entire entryway with a sixteen-foot banquet table. The door is unlocked so we let ourselves in.

The enormous table, actually four card tables pushed end to end and covered with matching periwinkle tablecloths, juts up to the front door.

Martha Stewart would surely approve of the yellow linen napkins with various pink floral prints and stripes, square glass vases filled with floating canary yellow chrysanthemums, and cheery red votive candles, although she might not be keen on the chairs, a mishmash of hand-me-downs and loaners from the neighbors.

"Sorry, we're all back in the kitchen and didn't hear you come in," says Sid, a tall, handsome twentysomething with black curly hair and olive skin. He's neatly dressed in a white T-shirt and black slacks with a white apron tied around his waist. "Come on back, and I'll introduce you to everyone."

The shotgun-style house is smaller than it looks from the outside. Both of us can't fit in the kitchen at the same time, so Brent stands in the hallway.

"This is Anne," says Sid, pointing out a willowy, fair-skinned brunette with a kind face, her hair tied in a knot. Like the rest of the crew, she's dressed in black and white with an apron tied neatly around her waist. "And this is the pastry chef, whose name you don't need to know."

Two of the other roommates are here with Sid and Anne, helping with plating, serving, and last-minute runs to the grocery store. The pastry chef, who lives across town, spends her days satisfying the sweet tooth of Washington's political elite. It's a relatively new gig, and she's concerned she'll be fired if word gets out she participates in a not-exactly-legal underground restaurant. The guests are sworn to secrecy.

Sid, a self-described "former government worker who now works in the private sector," is the watchdog of the group. Tonight is only the group's fifth dinner, so they're not yet comfortable with the legal ramifications of hosting a home dinner and charging a fee.

"We're not as concerned about the catering licenses and all of that," he says. "Anne and the pastry chef work professionally in the industry so they know what they're doing, and we don't make any money. But we can't risk people finding out . . . because of the tax implications."

It's the first time I've heard a nascent underground restaurant discuss taxes. Typically, those kinds of concerns develop later as an underground starts turning a profit and turns into a business with a catering or restaurant license. But this is D.C.

The pastry chef is hunched over a baking sheet, lifting the edges of caramel-colored *tuiles* (lacelike butter cookies). She's set herself up in the corner—essentially the hallway that spills into the kitchen—on a tiny, rickety wooden table. It's the only open space that isn't filled with the components of tonight's dinner in various stages of completion: coffee mugs filled with *panna cotta*, marinating game hens, a half-dozen chutneys and sauces. Anne is perfectly calm. Compared to the restaurant, tonight is a piece of cake.

"It's a little more chaotic because we only have our kitchen, so we're tight on space," she explains. "The last few dinners we've lucked out and borrowed our neighbor's kitchen, which is much bigger."

A few days before each dinner, Anne and the pastry chef coordinate work schedules so they can test recipes. Anything that doesn't pass the test is scrapped.

"Well, secretly we want them to test the recipes to make sure the leftovers are going to be good," jokes one of the roommates turned chef assistants.

Brent and I head back into the living room to mingle with the guests. It's largely a khaki slacks and smart skirt crowd in their mid- to late-twenties, the same age as the hosts. Half are friends or friends of friends, the rest curious foodies who heard about HUSH from a past guest.

"Is it OK if we just set our wine on the table?" asks Will, a former professor who works for Northrop Grumman and pens culinary history books in his free time.

A predinner cocktail is included in the $40 HUSH price, but it's BYOB during the meal. Naturally, I forgot to pick up a bottle of wine. HUSH doesn't stock extra bottles for forgetful guests (although this would be a good idea; I would happily pay a premium for any bottle that could be scrounged up). I dash to the wineshop on the corner, but it's already closed. Will kindly offers to share his bottle when I return empty-handed.

By the time I get back, all the guests have arrived and Sid has passed out tonight's cocktail, a crimson-colored mimosa made with lychee syrup and champagne. Anne likes to play with unusual cocktail combinations as much as she likes to play with food.

"I judge whether it's a winner based on how full the glasses come back," she says. "We did an oatmeal-infused vodka with fall spices that people loved, but then I tried steeping edible flowers and those came back half full."

From all the hugs and kisses it's clear several guests know one another, although unlike the other underground dinners I've attended, more than half arrive alone. It's a very friendly and diplomatic crowd, with formal handshakes and guests making an effort to work their way around the room, although the enormous table blocking the pathway makes it impossible to do much more than smile and wave from afar.

I toss back the last sip of my mimosa just as Sid announces dinner.

"Look for the place card with your name on it and take a seat," Sid politely instructs us, pulling out a seat for one of the ladies.

I've never had an assigned seat at an underground dinner, but it's a good idea. Not sitting next to the person you came with forces you to mingle with the other guests, part of the point of underground dining. Although it appears that Brent and I are the only party of two who aren't sitting side by side.

"We'll be coming around in a moment to open your wine bottles, but if you need anything else right now, please let us know," Sid continues.

In addition to being the watchdog, Sid acts as the HUSH restaurant manager, checking on guests, making sure the chefs have everything under control, and dealing with last-minute problems. Right now, the problem is tight seating.

Two men are sitting on either side of Brent, no small guy himself, making it impossible for him to scoot his chair close enough to the table. We switched seats, leaving Brent between Anne's sister and Carrie, a friendly brunette who works for a local nonprofit that aids children in Africa. And me next to Mr. Encyclopedia.

"Aloo Mutter, what's that?" Robert asks me, reading the back of the printed menu where each of the seven courses is described, just as Anne comes out of the kitchen to announce the first course.

"Tonight we're going to India for inspiration, a place I fell in love with when I lived there, especially the food," she says in a formal tone, the way I imagine she would address a group of guests at a private tasting at the restaurant. "Aloo Mutter is a very popular Indian dish with potatoes and peas; we used the same flavor combinations to create our own spin."

While Anne talks, the assistants place mismatched coffee mugs in front of each guest. Each is filled with a few spoonfuls of light green pea *panna cotta* topped with a pool of brick red tamarind sauce and a thick-cut homemade potato chip. It looks nothing like traditional Aloo Mutter, a homey hash of chunky potatoes and peas sautéed with tamarind and spices. Anne's version is beautifully presented, a detail you'd expect at the finest restaurants, although perhaps without the mug.

"Oh wow, this is incredible," Brent says as he bites into the custard-covered chip.

The earthy sweetness of the peas against the citrusy tamarind sauce is fantastic. By the time the assistants return to quietly whisk away our mugs, they've all been wiped clean.

"Lately I'm really into Wikipedia, and I've been writing a lot of their political factoids," Robert tells me. "Maybe you've seen some of them?"

Anne returns to announce the next course, Pani Poori, or Panipuri (literally water in fried bread), described on the menu as a crunchy puff filled with mint water.

"What does that mean?" asks Robert.

Anne describes the deep-fried pastry pillow filled with tamarind chili water, her favorite street snack in India. It has to be eaten immediately, before the tamarind liquid dissolves the pastry.

The servers set plates filled with paper-thin puffs and individual carafes of warm mint water—Anne's interpretation of the traditional tamarind water—in front of each guest. With a little guidance from Sid, we fill our puffs with the liquid and pop them into our mouths as quickly as possible before they dissolve.

"Oh wow, that's fun," says a diner at the opposite end of the table. "Yummy."

Next up is Bhel, also known as Behl Puri, another Indian street food made from puffed crispy rice and layered with tomato, onions, potatoes, green chilies, and spices and served with a sweet chutney. Anne's version includes puffed rice, duck fat–fried potatoes, tomatoes, and sweet cilantro chutney.

It sounds interesting, but the flavors don't quite work. But it doesn't really matter. Dining here is partly about participating in the experiment, watching a talented young chef explore her potential.

"The table linens are so adorable," says a museum educator at the opposite end of the table.

Helen and Steve brought the linens, silverware, and china from Philadelphia—a two-and-a-half-hour drive—after work. They belong to Helen and Anne's mom: pink- and gold-rimmed wedding plates, silver fleur-de-lys flatware, and china teacups. Helen and Steve are driving back tonight, too, although not until everything has been washed and neatly repacked in the antichip microfiber case to return safe and sound to Mom.

The fourth course, scallops in a spicy mango sauce on a bed of sautéed spinach, is fantastic. The scallops are perfectly cooked—tender and juicy. I'd order this dish at any restaurant . . . if only I could order a glass of chardonnay to go with it.

"I don't think I'm going to find this in Uganda," says Carrie, as Sid and crew set down plates of yogurt-marinated Cornish game hen with smoked eggplant.

Murghi, as it's called on the menu, is a spiced chicken dish typically cooked in a tandoori oven. Sid grilled tonight's version on the back porch.

"A toast," says a twenty-six-year-old senator-in-training who's been working the back half of the table all night. "I'd like to thank Sid and Anne and everyone else who worked so hard this evening for a fantastic dinner. And in case everyone doesn't know, I'd like to announce Sid and Anne's recent engagement. To Sid and Anne. Cheers!"

Anne turns beet red as we raise our glasses. Jelly, the puppy Anne and Sid recently adopted, pops out of the kitchen for the family moment, or perhaps it was just the smell of game hen.

Dessert is yet to come. Everyone is anxious to taste the delicacies of the top-secret pastry chef. But first the cleanse: a coconut *dacquoise* with coconut curry foam. It's a small round of tender coconut cake topped with diced fruit.

"Mmm," says Robert, scraping up the last bits. "This is really good." It is.

The crew whisks it away and sets down a second dessert, flourless dark chocolate cake with salted caramel popcorn and summer corn ice cream. It's one of the most unusual, and best, desserts I've had in a long time.

The senator-in-training rises again, wineglass in hand. "One more toast," he says. "To thank the talented pastry chef [says her name here] who prepared these amazing desserts and took time out of her busy schedule to cook for us."

Sid gives him a glare. "Oh no, I wasn't supposed to say that," he says, sincerely apologizing. "I completely forgot. Pretend you didn't hear that. But it's pretty cool where she works, right?"

The plates are cleared and Mom's lovely little china teacups reappear, this time filled with spicy chai tea. Envelopes with each guest's name are passed around the table. The price, listed on the menu, is $40—a bargain for the quality of the food, some of the most interesting I've had at an underground restaurant.

By now the chefs and assistants have joined us in the living room. They've tossed aside their aprons and have popped the champagne. Sid turns up the CD player and they trade serious faces for smiles, kicking back after dinner service just as they would at a restaurant.

Brent and I head for the door with the rest of the guests, thanking our hosts for such a lovely evening. Years from now, when Anne and the pastry chef are at the helm of their own James Beard-award-winning restaurants, we'll be able to say we knew them when.

RECIPES

Oatmeal on the Rocks

Anne suggests doubling or tripling the recipe so you always have oatmeal vodka on hand for drop-by winter guests. Oatmeal gives the vodka a subtle nutty oat flavor. Combined with the spices, honey, and apple juice, "it tastes like an oatmeal cookie in a glass," she says. Plan ahead; the infused vodka requires several days to make.

Makes 6 to 8 cocktails

10 ounces vodka

1 cup old-fashioned rolled oats

1 cinnamon stick

¾ cup honey

22 ounces apple juice

Ice

Pour the vodka into a large glass jar with a lid. Add the oatmeal and seal the jar. Set aside for 3 days, shaking once each day.

Strain the oat mixture through a cheesecloth-lined sieve. Repeat, if necessary, to ensure all the sediment is removed. Return the vodka to the jar (at this point, the vodka will keep up to 1 month). Add the cinnamon stick and honey, stir well, and let sit for 12 hours or overnight.

Remove and discard the cinnamon stick; add the apple juice to the jar. Shake or stir well and pour 4 ounces (for a rocks glass) or 6 ounces (for a martini) of the mixture into a cocktail shaker. Fill with ice and shake until chilled. If using a rocks glass, fill the glass with ice and strain into it, or pour directly into a martini glass. Serve immediately.

Sweet Pea Panna Cotta with Tamarind Chutney and Potato Crisp

Serves 8

Ice cubes for blanching

4 cups water, divided

2 teaspoons salt

2½ cups fresh or frozen peas

2 tablespoons butter

½ medium onion, finely diced

2 cloves garlic, minced

3 cups heavy cream

¼ teaspoon kosher salt

¼ teaspoon white pepper

1 packet (1 ounce) powdered gelatin

1 tablespoon cold water

Potato Crisps (recipe follows)

1 tablespoon butter

Fine sea salt

White pepper

5 tablespoons tamarind chutney

Prepare an ice bath by filling a medium bowl with 2 cups of the water and several ice cubes. Set aside.

In a medium pot, bring the remaining 2 cups of water to a simmer. Add the salt and peas. Simmer for 30 seconds and strain. Immediately place the peas in the ice bath, strain again, and set aside, reserving ½ cup of peas for garnish.

In a medium saucepan over very low heat, melt the butter. Add the onion and garlic and cook until translucent but not browned. Add 2 cups of the peas and the cream. Add the kosher salt and the pepper and cook for 2 minutes.

Transfer the pea mixture to a blender and puree until smooth. Strain through a fine-mesh sieve into the sauce pot (do not turn on the heat), pushing on the solids. Discard the solids. Taste, seasoning with additional salt and pepper if needed.

In a small bowl, sprinkle the gelatin over the cold water until rehydrated, about 2 minutes.

Warm the pea puree over medium heat and add the gelatin. Stir until completely dissolved, about 1 minute. Divide the mixture among 8 ramekins, teacups, or other serving containers. Refrigerate overnight.

Remove the *panna cotta* from the refrigerator 45 minutes prior to serving to come to room temperature.

In a small sauté pan, combine the reserved peas, butter, salt, and pepper. Heat over medium heat until just warm, about 1 to 2 minutes.

To serve, top each *panna cotta* with a dollop of chutney and sprinkle with the peas. Garnish with a potato crisp. Serve immediately.

Potato Crisps

The crisps can be made several hours ahead. If they lose their crunch, rewarm them in a 225° oven for 5 to 8 minutes, until crisp.

Ghee (Indian clarified butter) is available at Indian markets and well-stocked grocery stores. You will need 2 silicone baking mats to make these crisps.

8 tablespoons melted ghee or clarified butter, divided

2 Yukon gold potatoes

½ teaspoon table or fine sea salt

¼ teaspoon white pepper

Preheat the oven to 225°.

Line a baking sheet with a silicone baking mat and brush with 2 table-spoons of ghee. Slice potatoes horizontally as thinly as possible, about $\frac{1}{16}$-inch, using a mandoline or very sharp knife. Lay the potatoes on the baking mat, making sure none are touching, and brush with the remaining 6 tablespoons of ghee. Sprinkle with the salt and pepper and lay a second silicone mat on top.

Bake until the crisps are golden brown, about 45 minutes, rotating the baking sheet after the first 20 minutes for even cooking. Sprinkle with additional salt if desired. Let cool completely and serve.

Scallops with Spicy Mango Sauce and Pineapple-Mango Compote

Mango pulp is available at Indian markets and well-stocked grocery stores. Anne recommends making the sauce and compote ahead of time.

Serves 6

Spicy Mango Sauce (recipe follows)

Pineapple-Mango Compote (recipe follows)

¼ teaspoon fine sea salt

¼ teaspoon white pepper

2 teaspoons all-purpose flour

6 large sea scallops

1 tablespoon canola oil

2 tablespoons butter, melted

1 teaspoon fresh thyme leaves

In a small bowl, combine the salt, pepper, and flour. Sprinkle both sides of the scallops with the mixture and set aside.

Heat a large sauté pan over medium high heat and add the oil, tilting to coat the bottom of the pan. Continue to heat until the oil is hot, about 30 seconds; add the scallops. Sear until browned, about 1 minute. Flip and repeat until scallops are browned on the outside but still rare in the center. Lower the heat if necessary to prevent burning. Add the butter and thyme, stirring to coat the scallops.

To serve, place 1 generous tablespoon of mango sauce on each serving plate. Top with a scallop and a dollop of the compote. Serve immediately.

Spicy Mango Sauce

16 ounces pineapple juice

1 shallot, thinly sliced

1 clove garlic, thinly sliced

Juice of 1 small lime

Juice of 1 medium lemon

Juice of ½ medium orange

1 green chili, finely diced

½ cup mango pulp

½ stalk lemongrass, pounded

1 tablespoon plus 1 teaspoon honey

¼ teaspoon kosher salt

In a large saucepan, combine all the ingredients over low heat and simmer, stirring occasionally, until the sauce has thickened, about 2 hours. Season with additional salt to taste, strain through a fine-mesh sieve, and set aside. The sauce may be made up to 2 days ahead, covered, and refrigerated.

Pineapple-Mango Compote

½ cup finely diced pineapple

½ cup finely diced mango

¼ teaspoon chili powder

¼ teaspoon kosher salt

1 tablespoon olive oil

Combine all ingredients in a medium bowl and set aside. The compote may be made up to 2 days ahead, covered, and refrigerated.

Sweetbreads with Herb Gnocchi and Sage Cream Sauce

Anne suggests making gnocchi when you have some time. The sweetbreads and gnocchi can be made earlier in the day, reheated, and assembled just before serving.

Serves 6

Gnocchi (recipe follows)

Sage Cream Sauce (recipe follows)

Sweetbreads (recipe follows)

1 tablespoon canola oil

1 tablespoon shallots, minced

1 teaspoon garlic, minced

1 tablespoon butter

Heat a large sauté pan over medium high heat and pour in the oil, tilting to coat the bottom of the pan. When the oil is hot but not smoking, add the gnocchi and sauté, stirring occasionally until golden brown on all sides, about 4 minutes. Add the shallots, garlic, and butter and toss well.

Warm the sauce.

Divide the gnocchi among 6 serving plates and top with sweetbreads and sauce. Serve immediately.

Gnocchi

3½ cups water, divided

12 tablespoons (¾ cup) butter

2 tablespoons kosher or coarse-grain sea salt, divided

2 cups all-purpose flour

2 tablespoons Dijon mustard

1½ cups (4 ounces) Gruyère cheese, grated

3 tablespoons freshly chopped parsley

3 tablespoons freshly chopped thyme

3 tablespoons freshly chopped sage

5 eggs

Ice cubes for ice bath

5 tablespoons olive oil

In a large pot over medium heat, combine 1½ cups of the water with the butter and 1 tablespoon of the salt. Bring to a simmer and add the flour, stirring constantly with a wooden spoon. Continue stirring constantly for 5 minutes, beating out any lumps of flour, and lowering the heat if necessary to prevent the dough from browning. (You will have a flour film on the bottom of the pan.)

Transfer the dough to a stand mixer with a paddle attachment. Or, to use a handheld beater, transfer the dough to a large bowl. Add the mustard, cheese, parsley, thyme, and sage; mix on low speed until just combined. Add the eggs one at a time, mixing thoroughly between each. Fill a pastry bag with the dough, twist the end closed, and refrigerate for at least 1 hour and up to 24 hours.

Prep.are an ice bath by filling a medium bowl with the remaining
2 cups of water and several ice cubes.

Bring a large pot of water to a boil and add the remaining 1 tablespoon of salt. Pipe the chilled dough into the pot, using a knife to cut
off 1-inch nuggets. Cook until they float to the top; skim them off and
place them in the ice bath. Repeat until all the gnocchi are cooked.
Strain the gnocchi from the ice bath and place in a mixing bowl.
Immediately toss with the oil to prevent sticking. Set aside.

Sage Cream Sauce

2 cups plus 3 tablespoons water, divided

Ice cubes

1 bunch sage, leaves only

6 tablespoons cold butter

1 cup crème fraîche

Table or fine sea salt

White pepper

Prepare an ice bath by filling a medium bowl with 2 cups of cold water
and 3 to 4 ice cubes.

Bring a medium pot of water to a boil and add the sage leaves. Blanch
for 30 seconds and immediately add to the ice bath, and then strain
immediately. Puree in a blender until smooth.

In a small saucepan, bring the remaining 3 tablespoons of water to a boil. Whisk in 2 tablespoons of butter at a time, continually bringing it to a boil after each addition (this will emulsify the butter). Turn the heat to low and add the crème fraîche, stirring until incorporated. Remove from the heat.

With the blender running on the lowest setting, slowly pour in the crème fraîche mixture. Season with salt and pepper to taste. Prior to serving, rewarm for 2 to 3 minutes over low heat.

Sweetbreads

1 pound sweetbreads

½ teaspoon kosher or fine sea salt

¼ teaspoon white pepper

2 tablespoons all-purpose flour

About ½ cup canola oil

With a sharp knife, carefully remove the sinewy membranes from the sweetbreads by lifting them with the side of the knife. In a medium bowl, combine the salt, pepper, and flour. Toss the sweetbreads in the mixture and set aside.

Heat a medium sauté pan on medium heat and pour in ¼ inch of oil. When the oil is hot but not smoking, add the sweetbreads and cook, turning occasionally until golden brown on the outside and cooked through. Drain on paper towels.

SUB ROSA

Sub-rosa, adjective: Designed to be secret or confidential; secretive; private.

Sub Rosa comes from the Latin, literally "under the rose," from the association of the rose with confidentiality, in reference to the use of a rose at secret meetings as a symbol of the sworn confidence of the participants. The ceilings of ancient banquet-rooms were often decorated with roses to remind guests that what was spoken sub vino (under the influence of wine) was also sub rosa.

Anyone who is familiar with secret societies such as the Freemasons, Priory of Scion, Knights Templar or has read Dan Brown's book *The DaVinci Code* will be familiar with the concept of sub rosa. What goes on here, stays here.

The Sub Rosa restaurant began in a cottage on our property that was once the caretaker's quarters for a 90-acre orchard here in Dundee. Today Sub Rosa is morphing into a micro-distillery with culinary-infused vodkas, anejo rum, a wicked absinthe and other hand-crafted distilled elixirs.

—Sub Rosa

CHAPTER 6

"So what exactly is the equivalent of scratch and sniff on the Internet?" asks Meg Roland, a medieval history professor at a nearby liberal arts college.

The six of us sitting around Mike Sherwood and Linda Lausmann's patio table in the tiny wine country town of Dundee, Oregon, are entirely too enraptured by our salmon tartare to respond.

Tonight, for a handful of close friends and family, Mike and Linda's virtual underground restaurant, Sub Rosa, is real. Linda has been in the kitchen of their 1920s German cottage since the early morning hours preparing this evening's elaborate feast. Mike has already decanted a handful of bottles from the Sub Rosa wine cellar and is riffling through the CDs in his office downstairs—which doubles as Sub Rosa's in-house radio station—for the perfect music to set the tone. And I have the best seat in the house: a patio table facing the herb garden on a perfectly clear Oregon summer night.

"Linda, this is *way* too good. What did you put in here? Something illegal?" asks Dirk Jacobs, Linda's brother-in-law, as he heaps salmon tartare laced with fresh chives, tarragon, lime juice, and crème fraîche onto a toasted baguette round.

Dirk and his wife, Liz, Linda's sister, are fixtures at Sub Rosa dinners. They live a few miles away on a "gone amok old tree farm on top of a ridge overlooking Portland." Dirk works for an investment firm in Portland and volunteers as a local fireman on weekends. Liz spends her time revitalizing the farm: chopping and selling firewood, tending the grape vines and French "truffle trees" (trees seeded with French black truffle spores) they planted to qualify as a working farm so they could build a home on the site, and hosting Oregon tree farm-industry meetings.

"Yeah, I'm not quite sure how that happened," laughs Liz. "I'm just out there chopping down the dead trees on our property and the real tree farmers want to meet at our place. I called in Linda for food reinforcements—that always works."

Mike gets up to open another bottle of wine. "Feel that punt, it's enormous," he says, caressing the bottom of a 2001 Sineann pinot noir. Dirk and I reach over to feel the indenture in the bottom of the bottle.

"You know, you're the only stranger who's ever been invited to the *real* Sub Rosa," Mike informs me as he refills my wineglass.

"Ha!" yells Jerome Chicvara, a local brewmaster turned artisan distiller —and one of Mike's closest friends—sitting at the end of the table next to his wife, Meg. "Is that what these are called now, Mike? Sub Rosa?

I thought these kinds of things were just called dinner parties," he says, helping himself to more tartare from Meg's plate.

Although we have nice weather off and on during the spring, it's not like you want to eat outside at night without a jacket or a roaring fireplace nearby. And while summer here doesn't often kick into gear until after mid-July, if the spirit is willing and it isn't raining, we offer the option of eating outside at the cozy rustic outdoor dining room attached to the workshop and smokehouse or the romantic patio attached to the main house and strung with dreamy outdoor lights. In both locations, we have well-stocked fireplaces using wood from the property that add a rustic camp-like ambiance to your evening meal no matter what time of year it is.

The table is yours for the evening of course, but about 10 PM the early birds of the late night crowd start to show up for Sub Rosa's famous late night DJ scene and occasional live show. Check out our music page for a sampling of what has been spinning lately.

—Sub Rosa

Fifteen years ago, Mike quit his high-level job as a Seattle software executive and moved with his new bride to Oregon pinot noir country. With their savings Mike and Linda bought a German cottage, affectionately known as Casa Dundee, and pieced together a low-stress living, working part-time jobs and lingering over wine and food with friends. Most of the lingering happened in the kitchen.

Linda is a good cook, so good that friends begged them to open a restaurant. African peanut soup, Dungeness crab cakes with roasted pepper coulis, and apple tartlets with brandy crème anglaise weren't exactly easy to find in a town of greasy spoons and chain restaurants.

At first Mike and Linda humored the idea. They could turn their trellised, wildflower-lined garden patio into a drop-by café open for lunch and lazy weekend brunches. It would be the kind of place locals linger and passers-by pop in on a whim, complete with chalkboard menus, Linda's daily changing recipes, and organic fruits and vegetables Mike would pick daily from their garden. A wine country dream life.

But the reality of running a legitimate eating establishment—the permits, the inflexible hours, the curmudgeons bound to show up on occasion—ended Linda's visions of spooning marionberry ice cream atop French meringues for happy backyard customers. Instead, she took a part-time tasting room job at a nearby winery and satisfied her kitchen cravings by throwing elaborate dinner parties for their friends at Casa Dundee. While Linda was cooking, Mike bounced from an ever-changing array of gigs: Web consultant, brewery manager, distillery assistant, arts event producer, and for the past seven years, working at Sineann Winery.

"I love bringing in the fruit . . . the smells, the camaraderie, the late hours of rock and roll at the top of the hill. And once all the wine is in oak in November, everything is quiet at the winery except for the bubbling of the fermentation locks as the last of the sugar turns into alcohol. It's almost a Zen moment."

But getting to that moment requires months of backbreaking work, fourteen hours a day, seven days a week. It was after one of those long days at the winery, with Linda fast asleep and Mike icing down his swollen feet in his basement office, that Sub Rosa came to life.

It will come to as surprise to many that Sub Rosa has a clothing optional policy. We've been known to cook topless with only the benefit of a kitchen apron separating us from the flame. Nude barbecue, while not the rule, can happen on hot summer evenings at Sub Rosa.

This "tradition" started with our wait staff. It was late July—the week of the annual International Pinot Noir Celebration, and it was quite hot outside. We had to chill our Pinot Noir before serving because of the heat.

One wardrobe malfunction led to another that evening and soon the entire wait staff was topless. Being a huge wine tasting weekend, Sub Rosa was filled with out-of-towners including some French guests. There is something about being on vacation that releases the inhibitions. It wasn't long until half the female guests had doffed their tops as well. You would have thought you were at some French Riviera private

party, but no—just another magical weekend night at Sub Rosa in Dundee. . .

—Sub Rosa

Mike is showing me the stone talismans he's carved over the past thirty years: a rasta man with his best friend's wisdom tooth embedded in the back of the head, a modern-day Venus of Willendorf, a dancing turtle. "It works out my frustration. I've been doing it for years, but I've really cut back lately," he explains, rubbing a half-completed stone carving between his palms.

Recently, Mike has been working on a couple of new pieces in the Sub Rosa rock carving studio (otherwise known as a toolshed) out back: an erotic mortar and pestle and several crooked feet with knobby toes and bunions.

"Hey, my feet hurt," he says. "I'm not as young as I used to be."

"So how exactly are you going to find the truffles when they start growing?" Jerome asks Dirk. "Don't you have to have a potbellied pig or something to root them out?"

"Nah, I'll just make my wife find them," jokes Dirk. Groans around the table. "No seriously, we really don't know since we haven't seen them. Maybe they'll just appear. If not, I guess we'll ask some mushroom hunters or somebody at the Eugene Truffle Festival."

Mike gets up from the table to clear the appetizer plates and reappears with a tray of shot glasses filled with anise-scented liquor. This doesn't exactly appear to be the shot-tossing, table-slamming crowd.

"Mike, this one is good, better than the last, a stronger flavor—I'd go with it," says Jerome as he sniffs and sips.

The liquor is the final prototype for Mike's tarragon-infused vodka to be sold under his new Sub Rosa Spirits label, a project he's been working on the last few years. Getting into the distilling business isn't exactly easy. Home distilling is a federal crime, although beer- and winemaking are perfectly legit hobbies (Mike's done both and was bored with the home brew and wine scene). He's been working with a local distiller at an off site facility to make the tarragon vodka and a saffron version. "The initial blend needed a bit more toasted cumin for balance," says Mike. It was a 150-gallon batch.

"I was never as good at making beer as I am with spirits," he says. "With beer you have to be so precise and clean—orthodox Jewish clean—but with distilling you can make more of a mess, throw in this and that, and see what happens. I'm messy. Ask Linda."

When I visited, Mike was in the final stages of getting the Sub Rosa Spirits label approved. "They [the federal government] didn't like the phrase *light and refreshing* . . . the words *elixir* and *alchemy* are also verboten. They

allude too much to health potions and Harry Potter, I guess," he says. If all goes as planned, the distilling business will fund Mike and Linda's retirement. Those part-time winery gigs and nonexistent restaurants don't come with 401K plans.

Mike is fiddling with the CD player, loading a custom jazz mix he put together for tonight's dinner. Dave Brubeck's "Time Out" pipes over the outdoor speakers. Mixing CDs is one of his favorite pastimes—an outright addiction, if you ask Linda. In his basement office, he has three rows of shelving filled with hundreds of custom mixes. Friends often leave a dinner party with one, or all, of the evening's CDs in hand.

One night he'll mix up the James Bond theme song on the same CD with Britney Spears's "I'm Not a Girl, Not Yet a Woman" for his *Nude BBQ Mix: Soundtrack for Food, Beverage and Debauchery*. The next night it's Frank Zappa, ZZ Top, and the Foo Fighters together for *Bottling Line Music: Music to Rise Above the Din of the Bottling Line . . . Caution: This Rocks Out. Or Dueling Crab Cakes: Smackdown on the Turntable* with Johnny Cash and Frank Zappa duking it out over "Ring of Fire" or Bob Dylan and Guns N' Roses facing off with "Knocking on Heaven's Door."

It's an admittedly hodgepodge assortment of the most intriguing music from the past fifty-plus years of his life, all smashed together under one roof. "You'd think the DJ well would run dry. But no, there are always more tunes to come."

The music, like everything else at Sub Rosa online, is a glimpse into Mike's world. "If you look closely, you'll see the restaurant is really just my life, everything I love: the music, the food, Linda. Only not so blatant. I mean, does anyone out there really care about what we ate for breakfast, or that we have cute cats, other than Linda and me?"

Only, as soon as Mike opens the window, he draws the blinds. You're left to sort out what's real and what might just be a stretch of Mike's imagination.

Linda, known as Beef Girl to Sub Rosa fans, pulls a crepe torte with spinach Mornay sauce out of the oven. The nickname comes from Randal Huiskens's Zoom Comics featuring Beef Girl, who fuels her superpowers by consuming vast quantities of beef.

"You should see her put down a forty-eight-ounce rib eye," says Mike. "I'm more of a fish guy."

We take our seats on the patio. It's a crystal clear night, stars glistening in the moonlight.

"Now this is why I moved to Oregon," says Dirk as he sets down a platter of lamb and beef kebabs with local vegetables he's just pulled off the grill. "What a perfect night."

The lamb is marinated in a piquant combination of lemon juice, oregano, parsley, and sweet onion, and the beef kebabs in a tasty pinot noir, olive oil, thyme, and fresh rosemary marinade. But the crepes—two dozen paper-thin layers baked in spinach cream sauce—are getting all the attention. They'd make the perfect brunch dish—that is, if Mike and Linda ever reconsider the patio café.

"Well, I probably shouldn't have posted the GPS coordinates for our house online," says Mike, recalling one of many Sub Rosa fans irritated by the absence of a real restaurant. "But so far, no one has come knocking."

When Mike receives e-mails requesting dinner reservations, he clarifies that the restaurant is virtual and offers a few recipe suggestions. Most online fans find it entertaining, such as the special Valentine's menus he posted online, an all-meat menu as a tribute to his beloved Beef Girl and a seafood menu for himself. Although a few people still insist on making a reservation.

"When I told one woman that the restaurant was virtual, she said I was being socially irresponsible and deceptive, only in not such nice terms," he says. "You'd be surprised how literally some of these people take the Web site."

It might have something to do with the request for reservations and the words *prix fixe* plastered at the bottom of each menu.

"You don't have to drink your glass clean," says Mike, catching my glance as he opens the eighth bottle of the evening. "We're swimming in so much wine around here we could wash the floor with it. You can just taste it and spit it out—it's OK, really."

Online, Mike suggests wine pairings for each menu and Linda provides the recipes. Occasionally, he'll pipe in with his favorite recipes like a chai crème brûlée laced with Asian spices or the infamous Alice B. Toklas fruit fudge recipe (code name for pot brownies).

"The recipe isn't really on the site," says Mike. "But you'd be amazed how many people are directed to Sub Rosa for 'Alice B. Toklas brownies.' Internet searches for that and 'clothing optional' are two of our biggest hits."

Right, those nude barbecues he's been known to hold on hot summer evenings. It's summer, and it's pretty hot, but so far thankfully no clothing has been stripped.

"I can promise you, no guests have *ever* been nude in our home," Linda assures me.

"Linda keeps reminding me Sub Rosa is a family restaurant and I should be careful what I post," Mike says.

"I just don't want anyone to think he's a pervert with all those made-up ramblings. I mean take a look at him—he's not at all," she says, giving him a big bear hug.

"I'm a juvenile, what can I say? Too bad I killed all those brain cells in the '60s. Who knows what great things I could have done with my life," he chuckles.

We finish our salads—mixed greens with pancetta, goat cheese, and dried cranberries in a spicy vinaigrette—and move to the chairs near the outdoor fireplace. The conversation has tapered off to the occasional comment about a great wine or an upcoming food event. But mostly we just sit and stare at the stars, satiated and happy.

"Mike, can you come help me? I'm having technical difficulties with the ice cream. It's frozen solid!" yells Linda from the kitchen.

A few minutes later they appear with generous bowls of tangy-sweet crème fraîche ice cream topped with wild Oregon berries and a heaping platter of homemade hazelnut shortbread.

"Linda, this ice cream is amazing. And the cookies—wow," says Dirk, reaching for another. "The whole dinner has been fantastic, first-class as usual—can't wait until next time."

A reservation for two? No problem, a table is available anytime . . . online.

RECIPES

Salmon Tartare with Red Onion Crème Fraîche

You may substitute store-bought crème fraîche or sour cream lightened with whipped cream for the homemade version, but Mike recommends whipping up your own 24 hours in advance.

Serves 4 as a first course, 10 to 12 as a passed appetizer

> 1 cup crème fraîche, either Mike's Quick and Dirty Crème Fraîche (recipe follows) or store-bought
>
> Salmon Tartare (recipe follows)
>
> 2 tablespoons finely chopped red onion, rinsed and patted dry
>
> 1 tablespoon minced fresh chives
>
> ½ teaspoon kosher salt, plus additional
>
> ⅛ teaspoon white pepper, plus additional
>
> Crostini, toast points, crackers, or lightly toasted focaccia for passed appetizers

In a medium bowl, whip the crème fraîche with a whisk or handheld beaters until slightly thickened and beginning to form soft peaks. Fold in the onion, chives, salt, and pepper. Season to taste with additional salt and pepper. Cover and refrigerate until ready to serve or up to 24 hours.

To serve as a first course, divide the salmon among 4 serving plates and top with 2 tablespoons of crème fraîche. To serve as a passed appetizer, spoon 2 teaspoons of salmon onto each crostini and top with a dollop of crème fraîche. Serve immediately.

Mike's Quick and Dirty Crème Fraîche

Makes 2 cups

 1 cup chilled sour cream
 1 cup chilled heavy cream

In a medium bowl, whisk the sour cream and heavy cream together until incorporated. Use immediately or let sit at room temperature for a few hours to thicken slightly. Cover and refrigerate for up to 1 week.

Salmon Tartare

Choose the freshest sushi-grade salmon you can find. Mike rinses the white onion to remove some of its sharp bite, but if you prefer a spicier tartare, omit that step.

 1 pound fresh salmon
 3 tablespoons finely minced white onion
 1 clove garlic, minced
 1 green onion, including tender green stems, minced
 ½ cup finely chopped parsley leaves
 ½ cup finely chopped fresh tarragon leaves
 2 tablespoons olive oil
 1½ tablespoons fresh lime juice

Zest of 1 small lime

½ teaspoon kosher salt, plus additional

½ teaspoon white pepper, plus additional

Remove the skin from the salmon and discard. Using a sharp knife, mince the salmon until very fine. Do not use a food processor or the salmon will become mushy. Refrigerate while preparing the remaining ingredients.

Place the white onion in a fine-mesh sieve and rinse under cold running water. Press firmly with a wooden spoon to remove the excess water.

In a medium bowl, combine the salmon, white onion, garlic, green onion, parsley, tarragon, oil, lime juice, zest, salt, and pepper. Taste and adjust seasonings with additional lime juice, salt, and pepper, if needed. Cover and refrigerate for at least 30 minutes or up to 12 hours.

Mike's Sweet and Spicy Mango Chutney

Mike recommends starting with 1 teaspoon of cayenne and adding more to taste. He likes to serve this chutney with saffron-infused rice and *raita* (savory yogurt with fresh herbs) or alongside grilled lamb, beef, or chicken. This recipe makes plenty of chutney, enough to squirrel away for the winter or to give to friends.

Makes 2½ pounds

2 cups vinegar, divided

2 cups sugar

1 2-inch piece fresh ginger, peeled and sliced into ½-inch chunks

4 cloves garlic, peeled

2 pounds very firm mango, peeled and cut into ½-inch cubes

1 to 1½ teaspoons cayenne

1 tablespoon mustard seeds

2 teaspoons kosher salt

½ cup golden raisins

Set aside 1 tablespoon of the vinegar. Combine the remaining vinegar and sugar in a medium saucepan over medium high heat. Bring to a boil, reduce the heat, and simmer for 10 minutes.

Meanwhile, in a blender or food processor, combine the ginger, garlic, and remaining 1 tablespoon of vinegar. Grind to a paste and add to the saucepan. Simmer for an additional 10 minutes, stirring constantly.

Add the mango, cayenne, mustard seeds, salt, and raisins to the sauce-pan and simmer uncovered. After 10 minutes taste, and add a few teaspoons of vinegar if you like sour chutney. Continue to cook until the chutney has thickened, about 25 minutes total. Remove from the heat and allow to cool.

Refrigerate, covered, for up to 1 week, or pour into hot sterilized jars and seal, following manufacturer's preserving instructions.

Moroccan Braised Lamb

Mike serves this on a bed of saffron rice with his mango chutney folded into the rice and a dollop of chutney on the side.

Serves 6

1 tablespoon ground cumin

½ teaspoon ground cinnamon

½ teaspoon ground coriander

1 ½ teaspoons kosher salt, plus additional

½ teaspoon cayenne

½ teaspoon freshly ground black pepper, plus additional

2½ pounds trimmed boneless lamb shoulder, cut into 1 ½- to 2-inch pieces

4 tablespoons olive oil, divided

1 large onion, finely chopped

1 tablespoon tomato paste

2 cups low-sodium chicken or beef broth

1 cup dried apricots or a mixture of apricots, golden raisins, figs, and pitted prunes

2 large plum tomatoes, chopped

2 cinnamon sticks

1 tablespoon peeled, minced fresh ginger

2 teaspoons lemon zest

2 teaspoons honey

In a large bowl, combine the cumin, cinnamon, coriander, 1½ tea-spoons of the salt, cayenne, and ½ teaspoon of the pepper. Add the lamb and toss well to coat.

In a large heavy-bottomed skillet, heat 2 tablespoons of the oil over medium high heat. Add half the lamb and cook, turning occasionally until browned on all sides, about 8 minutes. Remove the lamb with a spatula, leaving the drippings in the skillet, and set aside in a clean bowl. Repeat with the remaining 2 tablespoons of oil and lamb and set aside.

Add the onion and tomato paste to the skillet drippings and reduce the heat to medium. Sauté until the onion is soft, about 5 minutes. Add the broth, apricots, tomatoes, cinnamon sticks, ginger, and zest and bring to a boil, scraping the browned bits from the bottom of the pan.

Bring to a simmer and add the lamb to the skillet. Reduce heat to low, cover, and simmer, stirring occasionally until the lamb is just tender, about 1 hour.

Uncover and simmer until the sauce is thick enough to coat a spoon, about 20 minutes. Add the honey, stirring well, and season with salt and pepper to taste. Serve immediately.

Hazelnut Zabaglione Semifreddo

This is Mike and Linda's favorite dessert, second to blackberry pie. You can make the zabaglione 1 month ahead and freeze it, and the chocolate sauce up to 2 days ahead, so it's perfect for entertaining.

Serves 6 to 8

    1 cup heavy cream, chilled

    6 tablespoons sugar, divided

    4 tablespoons water

    1¼ cups (4½ ounces) hazelnuts, toasted and skinned

    6 large egg yolks

    ¼ cup dry Marsala wine (do not use sweet)

    ¼ teaspoon vanilla extract

    Chocolate Marsala Sauce (recipe follows)

    ⅓ cup (1 ounce) hazelnuts, toasted, skinned, and coarsely crushed

In a medium bowl or stand mixer, combine the cream and 1 tablespoon of the sugar; whip to soft peaks. Cover and refrigerate until ready to use.

In a small saucepan, combine the water and 3 tablespoons of the sugar over medium heat. Bring to a simmer, stirring until the sugar is dissolved and the liquid is clear, about 2 minutes. Simmer an additional 2 minutes and set aside to cool.

In a food processor or blender, combine the hazelnuts and the remaining 2 tablespoons of sugar; grind to a paste. Set aside.

In a large metal bowl, whisk the egg yolks and wine. Set the bowl over a pan of boiling water (making sure the bowl does not touch the water) and stir constantly with a wooden spoon or heat-proof spatula until the custard has thickened slightly and reaches 160° to 165° on a thermometer, about 3 minutes. Do not let the mixture boil or the yolks will curdle.

Immediately place the custard in a clean mixing bowl or stand mixer and beat at medium speed until cool, about 8 to 10 minutes. Beat in the hazelnut mixture and vanilla until well incorporated. Using a large spoon, mix one-quarter of the whipped cream into the egg yolk mixture until well blended. Gradually add the remaining whipped cream, folding lightly until thoroughly incorporated.

Rinse 6 to 8 small ramekins with cold water. Do not dry. Set them in a small glass dish or plastic tub and cover with plastic wrap. Freeze overnight or up to 1 month. The zabaglione can also be frozen in a 1½-quart glass baking dish.

To serve: If you used individual ramekins, spread a pool of warm chocolate sauce on each dessert plate. Dip the ramekins into a bowl of hot water, loosening the edges with a small knife. Turn each zabaglione onto the sauce and sprinkle with the hazelnuts. Serve immediately.

If you used a large glass baking dish, transfer it to the refrigerator 2 hours prior to serving. To serve, scoop the zabaglione onto serving plates at the table using two large spoons. Sprinkle with the hazelnuts and the warm chocolate sauce.

Chocolate Marsala Sauce

½ cup water

1½ tablespoons instant espresso

⅓ cup dry Marsala wine

4 ounces bittersweet chocolate, preferably 70 percent cocoa, finely chopped

5 teaspoons sugar

2 tablespoons unsalted butter

In a small saucepan, bring the water to a boil and add the espresso. Stir until dissolved. Add the wine, chocolate, and sugar and immediately remove from the heat. Stir until the chocolate has dissolved. Cover and refrigerate for up to 24 hours. Rewarm over low heat, stirring constantly so the chocolate doesn't burn, and add the butter. Stir to incorporate and serve.

SUPPER
UNDERGROUND

~

SUG

Mixed Greens Salad with Texas Goat Cheese
and Fig Vinaigrette

Asparagus Soup with Lump Crab and Avocado

Scallop Cakes atop Wilted Spinach and Leeks
with Smoked Red Pepper Sauce and Mango Coulis

Chocolate Mousse with Fresh Berries

~

CHAPTER 7

"May I pour you a glass of wine?" asks the tall, hunky sandy blond as he picks up a bottle from the help-yourself wine table. "And I apologize, but tell me your name again?"

Mr. Handsome is wearing a perfectly pressed Ralph Lauren button down with khaki slacks . . . and sandals.

He pours me a glass of Spanish table wine. We swirl, smell, and sip. It's not very good, but we smile like it is. He tells me about his overseas adventures as an engineer for a Japanese manufacturing company. I wonder what his Tokyo colleagues think of a guy from Texas who wears sandals. He pours a second glass of wine—for his girlfriend—and politely excuses himself.

No matter; I'm not looking for a date. And neither is anyone else at Supper Underground (affectionately known as SUG), Austin's monthly roving underground dinner club. Most of the twenty-five guests have come with a spouse, friend, or date. A wise choice for underground dining, I'm learning. In a roomful of people you've never met, it's easier to grab a drink and survey the scene from afar with your companion than make small talk with strangers during cocktail hour. It's oddly counter to the reason many diners attend underground restaurants—to meet new people.

With no one to talk to, I busy myself reading the wine labels. They're the same bottles I saw on sale for $6 at the local grocery store this morning. The red is a basic Spanish table wine; the white, from Portugal, has a crustacean on the label and lively text promising it pairs beautifully with seafood. Was that an evil glance from Mr. Handsome's girlfriend and her cohorts? I'm probably just paranoid, but I flash my wedding ring her way in a gesture of peace.

Hannah Calvert, the founder of SUG and our hostess this evening, appears on the porch looking like a modern-day June Cleaver in a smart skirt and top with a pristine white apron tied neatly around her waist. She's classically pretty, a petite brunette in her early thirties with thick, shiny locks and a creamy complexion.

She sets down a large platter of tapenade-topped baguette rounds and surveys the scene. All appears to be in proper order, so she disappears back inside.

Tonight's dinner is in the backyard of a beautifully restored early twentieth-century Swedish-style home in east Austin. It's one of the last untouched historic neighborhoods within the city limits still devoid of million-dollar homes and designer lofts. Like most SUG host homes, this one is owned by a friend and former dinner guest. During most of the year dinners are held on patios and in backyards of private homes

throughout Austin with a "suggested donation" of $45 to $55, and most recently, $65. To avoid the Texas heat in the summer months, SUG moves indoors to restaurants, cafés, even the local grocery store—any place with an air conditioner.

"I'm very social, and I love being the hostess. It's such a great feeling," says Hannah. "I love seeing the new friendships that come out of our dinners. That's what makes this so rewarding."

Hannah moved to Austin from her native Virginia five years ago to attend graduate school in public policy. During the week she works as a public relations executive; on weekends she entertains friends or hosts SUG dinners for two dozen or so strangers. A good public relations executive knows how to make everything appear perfect, even when it isn't—just like a proper Southern hostess.

Tasso Ziebarth has his hands wrist deep in a bowl of chopped scallops. Officially, Tasso is SUG's chef, although Hannah points out that they plan the menus, shop, and cook together. After hosting two underground dinners on her own, Hannah called in Tasso for reinforcement. Planning a sit-down dinner for twenty-five people you've never met, cooking in an unfamiliar kitchen, and playing hostess at the same time is a little more complicated than throwing a casual supper for friends in your own dining room.

Tasso is a teddy bear of a guy in his early thirties with a contagious laugh, usually rambling on about this and that. "I always wanted to be a chef," he says, chopping onions on the cutting board he's learned to bring along. Cooking in someone else's kitchen means you have to come prepared. "But it took me a while to go there."

In 2001 Tasso moved to San Francisco. He started as a line cook at Aqua and worked up to the *garde manger* station (prepping items for the cold salads, raw bar, and charcuterie plates). But haute cuisine wasn't a good fit for a displaced Texan more interested in grilling a mean ancho steak than spooning caviar on chilled beet *verrines*. So he took a job as a line cook at Cajun Pacific, a New Orleans–style restaurant with plenty of jalapeño corn bread, barbecue shrimp, and grilled rib eyes to keep him happy for a year. Next was Café Marima, San Francisco's most authentic Oaxacan restaurant. But the Tex-Mex of his home state was calling, so he moved back to Austin. He worked briefly at South Congress Café and then decided to hang up his chef's jacket.

"Gotta pay the rent, you know?" he says, scooping up a heaping cup of onions and tossing them into the scallops. "So I got a practical job in finance. And then Hannah came to me about this underground dining thing she'd done a few times and it sounded cool. I get to cook here, do the stuff I really like, but keep my day job."

Tasso glances at the clock and tosses the scallop mixture into the fridge. He's running a bit behind, but judging by the cocktail buzz outside none

of the guests have noticed. Hannah instructs her two assistants, interns at her public relations firm, to prepare the plates for the mixed green salad. Tasso slices a log of local goat cheese and gives the fig vinaigrette a good shake. (The salad dressing, like many components for tonight's meal, was made last night and transported in Tupperware.) Each plate gets a handful of mixed baby greens, a few slices of cheese, and a drizzle of dressing. The salad is simple and easy to serve and requires very little cleanup. Perfect for a roving underground dinner.

Hannah and Tasso have learned it's best to serve dishes that involve limited on-site preparation. The first course is typically a soup (easy to make ahead and reheat, or better yet, serve chilled) or salad that needs only a simple garnish or splash of dressing. Main courses that can be finished in the oven, like tonight's scallop cakes, are ideal (so much, in fact, that this is the second scallop cake appearance recently). Desserts are homey, not fussy, such as tonight's chocolate pudding, an assortment of rotating homemade ice creams, and, in the winter, Tasso's favorite winter apple crisp.

Hannah heads outside to announce dinner. "Sit wherever you'd like, and please make yourself at home—we're so glad to have you here tonight."

One assistant lights the tiki torches wedged in the grass; the other lights the votives lining the white-linen-covered banquet tables. The tables and chairs are rentals; the plates, glassware, and silverware are Hannah's— easier to box up and toss in the trunk at the end of the night.

"We love food, we love to try new restaurants around town, so when we heard about these dinners we had to come see what they were about," explains Rose, an Austin Convention and Visitors Bureau employee in her midforties, and her husband, Adam, a self-described "little of everything kind of guy."

Like many guests, Rose and Adam heard about SUG from a recent posting on a local Web blog. As soon as SUG was listed as the hot new place to "walk away with full tummies and new friends," the mailing list more than doubled to six hundred people.

But with only one dinner per month and a twenty-five-seat capacity at most dinners—and several of those seats filled by the host homeowner and their close friends—getting into SUG can be tricky. In its earliest days, landing a reservation was like scoring concert tickets. After the specifics of an upcoming dinner were announced to the mailing list, the first twenty-five responders got in. But anyone who didn't happen to be online at the time of the announcement missed out, so Hannah and Tasso added a twenty-four-hour sign-up window. Now they use a lottery system to randomly select guests, and send congratulatory e-mails to those who get a reservation.

Scoring a seat at a SUG dinner, it seems, is part of the appeal.

Andy Brown, a young intellectual property lawyer turned Austin politician—and owner of tonight's host home—takes a seat at the head of the table and everyone else settles in around him. The standard underground dinner introductions go round: name, what area of town you're from, and how you heard about SUG.

Jimmy, the owner of a local interactive event Web site, grabs a bottle of wine from the middle of the table and tops off our glasses. "White or red?" he asks. He's referring to the same two labels from the bottles on the appetizer table, presumably a bulk purchase. By round two, they're not half bad.

Rose asks Andy about the house. "Well, it was a true fixer-upper, even the neighborhood, but I just feel like this is the next place to be in Austin—or at least that's what my real estate agent told me," he explains. "Once I got into the restoration, I couldn't stop. Let's just say I spent a lot more than I should have."

Only Andy doesn't live here. He rents an apartment in west Austin so he can run in that district for Democratic State Representative. He lost last year's nomination, but at barely thirty with plenty of good years of politicking ahead, he's not concerned. The lawyer currently renting his house also happens to be SUG's lawyer, a convenient source of legal advice in the never-ending quest by underground restaurateurs—at least those like Hannah and Tasso, who strive to function within the law—to operate legally. (Or eventually to operate legally, when business picks up and the health inspectors and tax collectors come knocking.)

Hannah pops outside under the guise of adjusting the CD player, but she's clearly here to check on her guests. We're hardly fifteen minutes into dinner and everyone is chatting like old friends. She looks pleased.

"How's everyone enjoying the salad? Isn't the goat cheese just wonderful? And that fig dressing?" she asks. Nods of approval go round the table. "Good, good. Well, if you need anything, let me know," she says with a smile, then disappears.

Actually, the salad could use a touch of salt. And a sprinkle of freshly cracked pepper would be nice. At a restaurant I wouldn't hesitate to ask for salt and pepper. But here, I don't want to hurt Hannah's and Tasso's feelings—I'm their guest, after all.

The assistants whisk away our salad plates and replace them with the second course, asparagus soup topped with a small mound of crab and diced avocado.

"Mmmm, this is really good," gushes Skylar, a friend of Hannah's.

"I think it needs a little salt," says Adam. Rarely have I seen salt and pepper—or a bread basket, for that matter—on underground restaurant dinner tables, particularly those that operate more like casual home dinner parties. "We've been to pretty much every restaurant in Austin, and we always check out the new places," says Rose. "We saw that write-up that raved about the food and had to come."

The write-up—the same blog that doubled SUG's mailing list—appealed to new SUG customers such as Andrea, a Texas Book Festival employee. She was drawn by the possibilities of meeting new people and enjoying good food in a unique social setting. But it also piqued the interest of foodies such as Rose and Adam, drawn more by the promises of "exquisite food" than the potential to make new friends.

Hannah and Tasso excel at creating simple comfort-food menus: spinach salad with bacon vinaigrette, pork roulade stuffed with goat cheese

and roasted vegetables, a warm apple crisp. It's relatively easy to prepare, easy to serve, and easy to like. After all, there's little point in turning out an expensive (and time-consuming) foie gras terrine if your guests would be happier with a steaming bowl of hearty corn chowder.

In the kitchen Tasso is putting the finishing touches on the main course. He slides a sheet pan of pan-fried scallop cakes into the oven and gives the sauté pan of spinach and leeks a firm shake. The mango coulis is waiting counter-side.

"Cool. We're almost there," he announces. In a few minutes all the entrées will be whisked away by the assistants, with only dessert left to plate.

Outside, the conversation has turned to the newest restaurants in Austin—which ones are worth a trip, which are best to drive on past. The servers set down the entrées and refill our wineglasses.

"Oh, now this I really like," says Rose.

The combination of sweet scallop cakes against the slightly bitter spinach and tangy-sweet coulis is a winner. And perfectly seasoned, too.

"You mean this isn't the only one of these kinds of dinners around? It's the first time I've ever heard of it," says a guy across from me, whom I have only now met. With twenty-five people at one table, it's easy to keep to conversations with your neighbor.

SUG began in early 2006, a few months after Hannah read a magazine article on an underground restaurant. Austin didn't have an underground dining scene, as far as she was aware, so why not start one? The idea of being paid to throw a dinner party—something she enjoys and does well—was too good to refuse.

But Hannah wasn't comfortable running anything illegal. So she contacted Jeremy Townsend, the underground restaurant hipster who founded the Ghetto Gourmet, for advice. He had transformed the Ghetto Gourmet from a small, truly underground (and illegal) San Francisco restaurant into a financially successful nationwide roving dinner club (translation: no more hiding from health inspectors or tax collectors).

In 2004, when Jeremy first started throwing dinners "to change the way we experience food, without walls and without boundaries," he hosted them in his apartment. Soon he was holding dinners several times a week for thirty to forty guests until a neighbor's noise complaint led local police to his door.

By holding fee-for-service dinners at his apartment night after night, he was technically operating an illegal restaurant. But according to the officer, if he changed the dinner location each night and asked for a "donation" rather than a set fee, it wouldn't be much different than a group of friends getting together for a supper club and splitting their expenses, now would it (wink, wink)? So Jeremy packed up his silverware and hit the road, holding dinners in host homes (typically previous dinner guests who donated their homes) throughout the country.

Hannah and Tasso have followed a similar model for SUG. Host homes are usually "donated" by friends or previous guests, reservations are made via e-mail, and payment for each dinner is a "suggested donation," not a required fee. Although the Ghetto Gourmet has since switched to an online payment system with advance credit card payment required—and therefore a traceable annual income—SUG remains a cash-only "donation" operation.

But as SUG has become more popular, they've been taking the legal steps necessary to turn the business into a legitimate legal entity, including applying for a catering license. They've also trademarked their name in the event of future, and presumably legal, expansions. According to the United

States Patent and Trademark Office, SUG isn't a clandestine restaurant. Instead, "Supper Underground provides social and entertainment activities in conjunction with catering services."

And those hot summer nights when SUG dinners are held in local restaurants, cafés, or even high-end grocery stores rather than backyards? It's not solely to beat the heat. They're all licensed food establishments, so it's perfectly legal for SUG—or anyone else—to rent them for dinner parties and charge a set fee, credit card payments welcome.

In the underground world, "success" (enough demand to raise fees and turn a profit) goes hand in hand with legitimacy (as eventually the IRS, and health inspectors, will come knocking) . . . and therefore the necessary licenses (typically catering) are often procured to make the operation legal.

In theory, whether a restaurant is legit shouldn't affect the diner's experience—other than knowing the restaurant isn't exactly underground anymore. But, higher prices often accompany the restaurateur's desire to turn a profit. And that means polite, forgiving dinner "guests" turn into paying customers with expectations. The $40 dinner that sounded like such a bargain for the quantity of food and wine is no longer such a great deal when it's $65. Suddenly, "How fun," becomes "I paid how much for *that*?"

"So what's the plan for after dinner? Y'all want to go out?" asks Warren, the lawyer who rents Andy's house, as dessert appears. It's billed as a chocolate mousse on the menu, although it's really more of a dressed-up dark chocolate pudding.

"Where are Hannah and Tasso? We've hardly seen them tonight," some-one at the opposite end of the table says. When they appear, we spontane-ously break into applause. Here, it seems oddly appropriate.

Thank-yous are exchanged, and Hannah makes a short speech about how much SUG means to them. We help ourselves to the last of the wine and get ready to leave.

"Please stay, enjoy yourselves," she says. "It's been so much fun, and we hope you'll come back. Oh, and the donation envelopes have been left on the table for your convenience." She and Tasso go back inside to finish cleaning up.

The donation is $50, not including tip. It's a bargain for the sheer quan-tity of food and wine (albeit cheap wine) and the quality of food we've consumed tonight, not to mention the hours of entertainment. I'd be hard pressed to find the same value at many Austin-area restaurants serving similar tasty, fresh fare. But relative to some underground restaurants that

charge the same—notably Caché and HUSH, where quality artisan ingredients are transformed into truly memorable meals—the price seems a bit steep. But then again, SUG is on its way to being a workable enterprise, and Caché and HUSH aren't in the business of making money . . . yet.

RECIPES

Wasabi Smoked Salmon Tartare

During the hot Texas summers, Hannah and Tasso like to serve cool appetizers and salads. Wasabi Smoked Salmon Tartare and Shrimp, Jicama, and Apricot Salad are two of their favorites for a large crowd. The tartare may be made up to 2 days ahead, chilled, and spooned onto the endive just before serving.

Serves 16 to 18 as a passed appetizer

¼ cup sour cream

2 teaspoons wasabi powder

1 tablespoon fresh lemon juice

¼ pound smoked salmon, finely chopped

2 tablespoons finely chopped red onion

1 tablespoon finely chopped fresh chives

3 to 4 heads Belgian endive, rinsed

In a medium bowl, mix the sour cream, wasabi powder, and lemon juice until well combined. Stir in the salmon, onion, and chives. Cover and chill for 1 hour or up to 2 days.

Cut off and discard the root ends of the endive. Separate the leaves. Spoon a heaping 2 teaspoons of salmon mixture on each endive leaf. Arrange in concentric circles on a large platter and serve immediately.

Scallop Cakes with Cilantro Lime Mayonnaise

These cakes can be made up to 12 hours ahead, chilled, and pan-fried just before serving.

Serves 8 as an appetizer, 4 as a main course

> Cilantro Lime Mayonnaise (recipe follows)
>
> Scallop Cakes (recipe follows)
>
> ¼ to ½ cup peanut oil, as needed

Remove the mayonnaise from the refrigerator 30 minutes prior to serving. Preheat the oven to 450°.

In a large skillet over medium high heat, heat the oil until very hot but not smoking, about 3 to 4 minutes. Fry half the cakes until golden brown on one side, about 2 minutes. Flip the cakes and cook another 2 minutes. Transfer to a baking sheet and repeat with the remaining cakes.

Bake until the cakes are firm and cooked through, about 7 minutes. Serve immediately with a dollop of mayonnaise.

Scallop Cakes

> 1 tablespoon olive oil
>
> 1 cup finely chopped onion
>
> 2 pounds sea scallops (any size)
>
> ½ cup chopped fresh chives
>
> 2 tablespoons chopped fresh parsley
>
> 2 tablespoons all-purpose flour
>
> 1 tablespoon peeled, minced fresh ginger

1 tablespoon fresh lime juice

1 large egg, lightly beaten

2 teaspoons kosher salt

1 teaspoon grated lime peel

¾ teaspoon ground black pepper

In a medium skillet, heat the oil over medium heat until hot but not smoking, about 2 minutes. Add the onion and sauté until tender and lightly browned, about 8 minutes. Set aside to cool.

Place the scallops in a food processor and pulse a few times until coarsely chopped (¼-inch pieces). Do not overprocess or the scallops will become gummy. Transfer to a large bowl and add the onion, chives, parsley, flour, ginger, lime juice, egg, salt, lime peel, and pepper. Form into eight ½-inch-thick patties, each about 3 inches in diameter. Place on a baking sheet, cover with plastic wrap, and chill for at least 1 hour or up to 12 hours.

Cilantro Lime Mayonnaise

1 egg yolk

½ teaspoon Dijon mustard

2½ teaspoons fresh lemon juice

3 tablespoons fresh lime juice

¼ teaspoon kosher salt, plus additional

¾ cup canola oil, divided

1 cup packed fresh cilantro leaves

1 clove garlic, peeled

¼ teaspoon hot sauce

In a food processor, blend the egg yolk, mustard, lemon juice, lime juice, and salt; process until smooth.

With the processor running, very slowly pour half of the oil through the feed tube until the mixture emulsifies and begins to thicken. Add the cilantro, garlic, and hot sauce and puree until smooth. Add the remaining oil and process until blended. Season to taste with additional salt, if desired. Transfer to a small bowl, cover with plastic wrap, and chill. Mayonnaise may be made up to 1 day ahead.

Shrimp, Jicama, and Apricot Salad

Serves 8

1 tablespoon kosher or sea salt, plus additional

1 pound large shrimp in shells (about 24), peeled, deveined, and halved lengthwise

¼ cup seasoned rice vinegar

½ teaspoon minced garlic

½ teaspoon minced ginger

2 tablespoons vegetable oil

1 pound jicama, peeled and sliced into strips ¼ inch wide and 2 to 3 inches long

1 seedless cucumber, peeled and sliced lengthwise into strips ¼ inch wide and 2 inches long

4 large apricots, cut into ¼-inch wedges

¼ cup chopped fresh cilantro

Freshly ground black pepper

Bring a medium saucepan of water to a boil. Add the salt and shrimp, stirring occasionally until the shrimp are opaque and just cooked through, 1 to 2 minutes. Drain in a colander and spread on a large plate to cool.

In a medium bowl, whisk the vinegar, garlic, ginger, and oil until well combined. Add the cooled shrimp, jicama, cucumber, apricots, and cilantro and toss well to combine. Season with additional salt and pepper to taste. Serve immediately or chill, covered, for up to 24 hours.

Tasso's Apple Crisp

This is a simple, classic crisp that's as easy to make as it is delicious. Cozy up around the fireplace and serve it with steaming cups of mulled apple cider.

Serves 8

> 7 Granny Smith apples, peeled, cored, and sliced
>
> 4 teaspoons fresh lemon juice
>
> ½ teaspoon vanilla extract
>
> 1 cup brown sugar
>
> ½ teaspoon ground cinnamon
>
> 1 cup old-fashioned rolled oats
>
> ½ cup (8 tablespoons) butter, at room temperature
>
> 1 pint vanilla ice cream (optional)

Preheat the oven to 350°. In a large mixing bowl, combine the apples, lemon juice, and vanilla, tossing well to blend.

In an 8- by 8-inch glass baking dish, slightly overlap the apple slices in neat rows to form layers. Continue layering until all slices are used.

In a medium bowl, combine the brown sugar, cinnamon, and oats. Add the butter, blending well. Sprinkle the mixture over the apples and bake for 45 minutes or until the apples are tender and the topping is crunchy.

Cut into 8 squares and serve with a dollop of ice cream.

UNDERGROUND, INC.

~

UNDERGROUND, INC.

Amuse: Smoked paprika foie gras pâté, preserved lemon zest, red currant gastrique, sea salt crackers.

Soup: Strawberry, Tellicherry crème fraîche, basil, orange blossom caviar.

Salad: Watercress, oven-cured zebra tomatoes, duck sausage, Fourme d'Ambert, honeycomb, aged sherry vinaigrette.

Fruits of the Sea: Avocado pâté, lump blue crab, grapefruit foam, smoked sea salt; Coriander-cured sockeye salmon, pickled mango, mint, red onion roll; Vanilla olive oil–poached scallop, grilled peach, grated botargo.

Intermezzo: Meyer lemon–Thai basil popsicle.

Birds of a Feather: Spanish fig–stuffed quail, foie gras, pine nuts; Curried cauliflower puree, asparagus, Marsala duck glace.

Dessert: White chocolate Bavarian and lavender mousse, liquid passion fruit.

~

CHAPTER 8

Breaking news . . . There's a new chef in town, and he's serving up some crazy good concoctions: green papaya salad with green bean emulsion and roasted peanut shrimp chips; saffron crème-poached Diver scallops with sun-dried tomato marmalade and vanilla *glace de veau* (concentrated veal stock); date tartlets with triple-cream Brie ice cream, raspberry vinegar reduction, and sherry foam.

Vegetable emulsions and vinegar-scented foams may be old news in cities flush with James Beard-award-winning chefs and multimillion-dollar restaurants. But I'm in Des Moines, Iowa, known more as caucus central than as a gourmet food mecca.

It's not that Des Moines doesn't have its share of foodie-friendly neighborhood bistros, upscale restaurants, and artisan food purveyors. But tonight's dinner guests have assured me the corn muffins at the local diner don't come with a sweet-cream honey butter watermelon chaser, the downtown steakhouse would never think of rubbing flatirons with licorice, and homemade peach bubble gum has never made an appearance in a cafeteria mint bowl. That is, until twenty-eight-year-old Hal Jasa came (back) to town and founded Underground, Inc.

"Twelve dollars," the cab driver says as he lets me out in front of the Cottage Bed & Breakfast. It was at least a half-hour drive from the airport.

"Welcome to Des Moines," he says.

Technically, the B&B is in the Drake neighborhood district, filled with turn-of-the-century homes, lemonade stands, and farmers markets in church parking lots. But it's more on the peeling-paint and sagging-roofline edge of the district—the B&B noticeably the only home on the block with a white picket fence and gurgling garden fountain. I ring the doorbell and the owner, with a diaper-clad two-year-old on her hip, opens the door. The smell of stale cigarette smoke and bacon grease is thick. "Hal and his people will be here any minute."

Hal has hosted more than a dozen dinners in the Cottage backyard. The owner often rents the space for private events, which means that supplies like chairs and banquet tables are easy to come by.

A beat-up pickup truck with a homemade charcoal gray paint job roars into the driveway and sputters to a stop. Hal jumps out, sporting a ripped black T-shirt, jeans, and a brown beret. He trots to the passenger door, pulls out an enormous cooler and an ice pop–filled cardboard box, and kicks the door shut.

"We know the space, and we know how to make it work. And there's a big grill, which is key," Hal says, explaining why he likes to host dinners in the B&B's backyard. "It's worth it to rent a place you know." After one dinner at a gutted penthouse—no oven, stove, or electricity, and the closest bathroom four flights below—Hal reconsidered exactly how roving Underground, Inc., should be.

"I thought it would be cool. But the ladies didn't find the bathroom hike in heels particularly appealing. And cooking a seven-course meal on four Bunsen burners didn't make for what I'd call a successful dinner," he says.

Dinner starts early in Des Moines, with cocktail hour at 6:00 sharp. Jessica and Susie, tonight's servers and back-of-the-house assistants, have been here since 3:00 polishing wineglasses and tossing around the local gossip. They've set up a worktable on the small brick patio to serve as the evening's hub for mixing cocktails and piling dirty plates.

"We get to hang out, work with Hal, who is just so *cool*, by the way, and eat the food," says Jessica, a restaurant hostess in her midtwenties who met Hal a few weeks earlier through a mutual friend. "I mean really great food, things I've never tasted before, like the first time I had foie gras custard, I just couldn't believe the flavors. Hal is just *amazing*."

"Well, some of us have had foie gras custard before," jokes Susie, a coordinator at a medical research firm and Hal's childhood friend. "I've traveled all over the world, you know, and we just don't have the diversity of food here. Hal's dinners are the only place I get to taste flavors I had in Vietnam or on Martha's Vineyard."

When Hal was just getting Underground, Inc., started, he relied on a friend's backyard and volunteers like Susie, paying them in cheap beer and a free meal. Now, he pays cash.

Crystal, the kitchen assistant, is slicing fresh honeycomb in the kitchen. She's a tough, no-nonsense type, a former line cook and Hal's go-to kitchen assistant. When twenty-seven hungry diners with high expectations sit down at the dinner table, it pays to have a professional by your side.

Hal isn't thrilled with the number of guests tonight. His ideal is sixteen, maybe twenty on a special occasion. Any more and the atmosphere changes from chef's table to catered event. But he didn't want to leave any of his loyal customers—or his mom—off the guest list because tonight is the last Underground, Inc., dinner. "It's been a great ride, the last sixteen months," he says. "I couldn't cook like this in a restaurant, at least until I have my own. But even with catering on the side it's a tough gig, with dinners twice a month. A lot of work and not much money. And the wife has a new business, so I've got to make consistent dough for a while, ya know?" His wife, Amber, has just opened a hair salon in town. "But Underground, Inc., will be back, in some form or another, one of these days."

Hal's new gig at Dos Rios, a three-hundred-seat upscale Mexican restaurant debuting in downtown Des Moines in one month, starts on Monday at 8:00 AM sharp. The buzz around Dos Rios has been building ever since Hal was named opening Executive Chef, and some of the restaurant's feature ingredients, such as homemade duck chorizo with tequila glaze, have hit the local food blogs. But he recently learned the restaurant owners hired a "culinary director" who will be designing the menu, so he's less than thrilled. "At least it lets me pad the pocket for now and build my own [restaurant] a little sooner."

Tonight he's going to pull out all the stops for his final meal. And his new boss will be here, too.

"Hal has always done his own thing," says his mom, Sharon Dowd. "He's always been creative."

Hal's not so sure his first job in magazine sales (or "cold-calling hell" as he describes it) would qualify as creative, but the sheer boredom of it turned his life around. When the company transferred him to Fort Worth, Texas, a friend asked if he wanted to be a food runner (one level above dishwasher, two rungs below waiter) at a local restaurant.

"Texas changed him," says Sharon. Between jobs at a country club and local chophouse, he worked at local chef Tim Love's restaurant, Lonesome Dove. It was in that kitchen he first tasted creative cooking: seared foie gras tacos with tomato jam and caramelized poblano peppers; spicy potato rösti with rabbit-rattlesnake sausage and red onion crème fraîche; coffee-cocoa-crusted pork tenderloin with purple chipotle mashed potatoes and braised garlic sauce.

"I could cuss, I could wear whatever the hell I wanted, and I got promoted three times in four months," he recalls. "Hey, I'm pretty damn good at this."

But Texas wasn't home. Hal returned to Des Moines to cut his culinary teeth at the Iowa Culinary Institute. Between semesters, he traveled around France and Italy, where he procured a taste for foie gras foam and home-made pancetta.

"The new culinary school in town has really changed the food scene in Des Moines," says Sharon. "These local kids go abroad and are exposed to foods and cooking techniques they haven't seen around here. Eventually they come back home and filter that knowledge through the community."

But the restaurant scene in Des Moines wasn't quite ready for a crazy kid like Hal behind the stove. "Everyone told me when I came back to Des Moines that I couldn't cook the kind of things we were serving in Fort Worth. So after school I started with dinners in my buddy's backyard. After one or two, word got out, and here I am," he says, tasting the lemon thyme muskmelon martini Susie handed over for his review. "But I don't think a lot of chefs in town have been happy to see me doing this. I'm pretty much disliked by other chefs but loved by the public, I guess."

And does the health department share the love?

"This inspector came to a restaurant where my buddy worked and asked if he knew the jerk that runs the underground restaurant," says Hal, looking pleased with himself. "The inspector was half joking, I think. They don't really care. I'm not open often enough to get them sniffing around. I sell food and liquor, but none of it individually, so it's a donation, really."

A $125 prepaid fee that includes cocktails and a six-course meal paired with wine doesn't sound much like any donation I've ever made.

"What the hell, who cares anyway, right?" says Hal, smiling.

But he does care about some things. He's careful to request food allergy information when he accepts a customer's e-mail reservation request and again when he confirms payment.

"I had five people at one dinner announce they're vegetarians when they walked in the door when we had ten meat courses. Now that's something I can handle. But the last thing I need is someone going into a peanut fit."

And it might get the health inspector to come knocking.

"Showtime," announces Hal as he rolls up the sleeves on his pressed black chef's jacket to reveal the life-size ten-inch chef's knife tattoo on the underside of one arm, a blue and red flame on the other. He turns up the jazz music and disappears to smoke a cigarette.

The first guests are milling around the long banquet table set up on the grass and commenting on the funky flower arrangements in stone-filled vases. Susie shakes up pitchers of martinis, and Jessica readies them on her tray.

By 6:15 everyone is here except Hal's future boss. It's a sport jacket and summer sundress crowd, mostly in their midthirties to midfifties, noticeably lacking in the twentysomething crowd prevalent at many underground dinners. I suspect the $125 price tag in a city where a steakhouse splurge will set you back half that amount has something to do with the age range.

"Shit, who are the suits? I think it's the people I told yesterday they couldn't come because there isn't room. I'm not going to have enough quail. Susie, they're gonna have to leave," says Hal, pacing around the grill. "You guys got it under control? I need another cig."

The uninvited people are B&B guests, politicians mainly. "Pardon me, do you know how to get to the 801 Steakhouse?" asks one as he heads out the back gate.

Crystal is focused on plating the *amuse*, a smoked paprika foie gras custard with red currant gelée. She sets out twenty-seven wood planks, one of the half-dozen serving dishes Hal brought, and she places a chilled shot glass filled with custard and a homemade sea salt cracker on each.

"You learn real quickly to bring things that transport well," says Hal, pulling shot glasses out of the cooler.

Hal follows behind Crystal with a plastic tub of currant gelée and a pinch of preserved Meyer lemon zest. He makes the preserved lemons, like almost everything else for tonight's dinner, at home. "My fridge is filled with jars of pickled and preserved everything. I'm also into curing right now—salmon, beef, whatever. And making caviar."

We're having one of his homemade caviars tonight, an orange blossom version served on top of a savory strawberry soup with Tellicherry pepper crème fraîche. The caviar is actually flavored gelatin Hal shapes into tiny spheres encased in taut skins so they literally burst in your mouth. The caviar-making experiments occur in his mom's kitchen, where there is plenty of room for unexpected explosions.

"That bubble gum caviar was a real mess, sticky gum everywhere," Sharon recalls. "It just destroyed my kitchen. But he's always good about cleaning up."

"You got this handled?" asks Hal, handing Crystal the gelée. "I've gotta do my bullshit speech—they're waiting."

Hal clinks a wineglass to get our attention. "Welcome to the last supper," he says. "All of you already know this is the end of the line, at least for a little while, so I've got my mom here . . . Mom, raise your hand . . . and my aunt, and my redheaded cousin, and his girlfriend even got dragged out . . . the rest of you, well, I'm not very good with names. But thank you for your support over the past year and a half. I put a lot of thought into tonight's menu, and I think it turned out pretty well. I hope you enjoy it. Enough talk, let's eat!"

With that, Hal saunters back to the temporary outdoor kitchen on the opposite side of the backyard. Susie and Jessica pour the first wine, a 2006 Spinyback sauvignon blanc from New Zealand.

"Oh good, it's white," says Hal's aunt, Dee Dowd, wiping the beads of sweat from her forehead. "It's so hot out."

I'm sitting at the middle of the banquet table, Hal's mom and aunt directly across from me, a friendly young lawyer, David, and his wife on my right. The rest of the table is made up of long-standing customers, a few family members, and that future boss.

"I hope he likes the dinner," jokes Hal. His boss has never been to an Underground, Inc., supper. "No pressure there, right? I hope he doesn't renege on the job offer."

The foie gras custard topped with the gelée is fantastic. Every shot glass is wiped clean.

"Let's ask for more of these crackers. They're great," says a gentleman sitting to my left.

"You can't do that here," his wife informs him. "It's not like a restaurant. I don't think they have extras."

The savory strawberry soup with the orange blossom caviar is a gorgeous crimson color, served with a dollop of cream and orange caviar artfully arranged between slivers of basil.

"This is weird," whispers the cracker fan.

It is odd. The caviar is intriguing, but the soup doesn't quite work. I take a few obligatory bites—sitting at the chef's table (which translates to the entire dinner table here) means the chef's watchful eyes (and tonight, his mother's) are on you as you taste every dish.

"Oh, you didn't eat much. Shall I leave that for you?" asks Susie, politely. I tell her it was fabulous, but I'm saving room for the next course.

"You've *got* to tell them the turkey story," Sharon begs her sister as the soup bowls are cleared.

Dee turns beet red. "Oh, I can't," she says, prompting everyone to encourage her.

"Well, OK," says Dee. "A few years ago, my neighbor who farms turkeys in her free time knocked on the door and asked me if I'd like a turkey for Thanksgiving—she had a few more than usual and needed to get rid of them—so I said sure."

A couple of days before Thanksgiving, a large, fully dressed fresh turkey showed up on Dee's doorstep.

"This thing weighed forty-two pounds," she says, arms open wide to show us the size. "Big birds are great and all, but what the heck am I going to do with a forty-pound turkey? She's a bit of an overachiever, this woman, and started the birds a month too early, so they got ridiculously fat. I couldn't find a single recipe in any cookbook that said what to do with a forty-two-pound bird. They all stopped at twenty-five. I tried to shove one in the oven, but the door wouldn't close. My other neighbor tried to cook one and it burned the knobs right off her oven. And she gave me three of them, all forty-pounders."

"That's 120 pounds of bird," Sharon adds.

Jessica and Susie set down the next course, watercress salad with twelve-year-old sherry vinaigrette, oven-roasted zebra tomatoes, duck sausage, blue cheese, and local honeycomb. They refill our wineglasses, this time with a 2005 Four Vines Naked chardonnay from Santa Barbara, and head back to the outdoor kitchen.

"So what happened to the turkeys?" asks David.

"Oh, we chopped them up and passed them around the family. Everyone cooked them at home and brought them to dinner," says Dee. "They actually turned out really nice."

The conversation lulls as we dig into the salads. "This is really good," says David. "Wow, honeycomb and sausage. Who would have thought!"

Sharon is beaming. "Hal really is a talented chef. He just continues to amaze me. You never know what flavors he's going to put together next. I'm not sure about that strawberry soup, but usually he's on target."

"And the cheese in the salad is Maytag blue, from around here of course," says Dee. "I'm trying to get my son to like it, being a local and all, but he's not very fond of the strong flavor. But if I freeze it in thin slices, he'll eat it straight from the freezer. It's more like ice cream that way, a neighbor told me, and not as strong. She's right."

Up next is a trio of dishes Hal calls "Fruits of the Sea." He's fond of simply listing ingredients rather than naming dishes or describing them in detail. They arrive on a long rectangular white plate, with each small bite artfully arranged in its own square dish. I take a bite of the first: avocado pâte, lump crab, ruby red grapefruit foam, and smoked sea salt. Foams aren't typically my favorite, often more about shock value than pure flavor. But here, it works. The essence of the grapefruit is perfectly balanced by the crab and pinch of smoked salt. The second small bite features Hal's cured salmon

made with a brown sugar-spice cure. Sliced paper thin and wrapped around a two-inch rectangle of pickled mango and red onion, it's fantastic. The third, a vanilla-infused, olive oil-poached scallop with a grilled peach slice and grated Bottarga (dried salted tuna roe) is even better.

On their own, each of these nibbles is worthy of an appearance at a top restaurant. Together, it's hands down the best dish I've had at any underground restaurant, rivaling the best dishes I've had at a "regular" restaurant, even. It's exactly what I expect from an underground restaurant, yet so rarely have found.

"Did you see the butter sculptures at the fair?" Sharon asks David and his wife. The Iowa State Fair is wrapping up this weekend. "They're pretty good this year, much better than last. There's a Harry Potter, too."

Hal reappears with the Meyer lemon–Thai basil frozen ice pops he carted over in his truck earlier this afternoon.

"A little tang for a palate cleanser," he says, offering them straight from the plastic mold.

"You've got to ask for extra ancho in the icing," says the lawyer's wife, referring to the new cupcake shop in town. "It was really spicy when they first opened a few months ago, but they've dumbed it down lately."

While they opine over the best new bistros and artisan purveyors in town, the opposite end of the table is discussing the finer points of sausage making. "She won't let me use the rabbits and squirrels in our yard," jokes a laid-back, long-haired man in his late thirties at the head of the table. His wife rolls her eyes. "That's gross, don't tell them that!" she says. "They might believe it!"

It's starting to get dark, so dark it's impossible to see the next course—Marsala-glazed quail stuffed with Spanish figs, pine nuts, and foie gras. It's served on a bed of cauliflower puree with asparagus tips. The local wine store salesman (and Hal's sommelier) chose a 2005 Twenty Bench Napa Valley cabernet to complement the heady flavors.

"Oh shit, what's that?" yells one of the guests, her hand under the table. Pumpkin, the neighbor's twenty-pound strawberry blonde Persian, is rubbing legs under the table, hoping for a bite of quail.

"First time he showed up, he ate all my lardons," says Hal. "So the next dinner, I brought two squirt guns to shoo him away, and he just rolled over on his belly and looked at me."

The quail is excellent, only I can't see it well enough to cut the meat from the bones. A couple of guests pick up the bird and start nibbling.

"Mama, how was the quail?" asks Hal.

"Great," she says. "I haven't had quail like this since your dad shot 'em and brought 'em home."

"Yeah, well with these you don't have to pick out the BBs!"

"Oh, ice cream," says the sea salt-cracker fan across the table, eyeing the mounds of creamy ice cream atop a half sphere of ice that Jessica and Susie have set in front of us. "Perfect." It's still pushing 90 degrees outside, and we're all glistening with sweat.

But the creamy mound is actually white chocolate and lavender mousse with an odd, grainy texture and a temperature that rivals that of the outside. The sphere of "ice" is a decorative sugar mold, and the "liquid passion fruit" inside the mousse is a chunky sorbet. It tastes more like a food science experiment than the perfect ending to an incredible meal. "Pastry hasn't been Hal's strong suit," says his mom as we set down our spoons. "But usually he does surprisingly good things with sugar. This one I'm not so sure about." The other guests nod in agreement. Maybe next time we'll be able to taste one of his signature sweet and savory desserts, like Cabrales cheese ice cream. Only there won't be a next time.

"It's really too hard to put on such elaborate dinners a couple times a month and try to make a living," explains Hal. "I'm not willing to sacrifice the quality of the food. But with only twenty guests, after I pay everyone—the location, servers, and my vendors—there isn't much left."

Hal hasn't completely given up on running a top-quality underground restaurant. He's thinking about redirecting the dinners into sustainable suppers using leftover farmers market produce. "So much gets tossed," he says. "And it's still excellent produce. So I'm thinking that maybe I'll start

a nonprofit, serve up great food, and support the farmers. Or maybe I'll open my own restaurant. That would be cool, too."

The idea for a new Underground, Inc., hasn't been fleshed out completely. In the meantime he'll be plugging away at his new job, waiting for the right moment.

Susie and Jessica pass around porcelain cups filled with rose tea. Sharon brought the rose blossoms back from a recent trip to China. She's been doling them out a few tablespoons at a time, to family only, because when they're gone, they're gone. But Hal's last supper is a special occasion.

"And they're supposed to help you lose weight," she assures the table.

We drink every last sip.

Postscript: Three months after Hal started working at his "real" job at Dos Rios, he quit: "We decided to part ways realizing my creativity far exceeds the long-term goals of the restaurant. So there is only one thing left for me to do: *go underground*." Stay tuned.

RECIPES

Lemon Thyme Muskmelon Martini

Muskmelons are industry code for cantaloupe, but you can use any variety of sweet, peak-of-season summer melon. The vodka must infuse for 1 week prior to using, so plan ahead. The recipe yields "enough to have a great evening," according to Hal.

Makes 25 small (3-ounce) cocktails

- 1 large bunch lemon thyme
- 1 750-ml bottle vodka
- 1 muskmelon (any variety), seeded and diced into medium chunks
- 1 bottle sparkling white wine such as Prosecco
- Ice

Place the lemon thyme in the vodka, reseal, and set aside for 1 week. Strain out the lemon thyme and return the infused vodka to the bottle. The vodka will keep, sealed, for several months.

Puree the melon in a blender until smooth and place in a clean bottle or large plastic container. Add the vodka into the puree and mix well.

In a cocktail shaker, combine 2 ounces of vodka with 1 ounce of sparkling wine. Fill with ice and shake until chilled. Strain into a martini glass and serve.

Steak and Eggs with Creamy Leek Potatoes

This is one of Hal's favorite dishes. The key, he says, is cooking the Wagyu at a lower temperature than is typical to keep the prized fat in, not dripping out of, the steak.

Serves 4

½ cup (8 tablespoons) plus one tablespoon butter, divided

2 large leeks, white part only, thinly sliced

¼ cup dry white wine

4 large baking potatoes, scrubbed and very thinly sliced
(use a mandoline if possible)

1½ cups heavy cream

¼ cup grated Parmigiano-Reggiano cheese

3 teaspoons smoked paprika

½ teaspoon kosher salt, plus additional

1 teaspoon freshly ground black pepper, plus additional

4 Wagyu beef New York strip steaks, 4 to 6 ounces each

4 duck eggs (or small chicken eggs may be substituted)

Preheat the oven to 350°.

In a large sauté pan, heat the ½ cup of butter over low heat and add the leeks. Cook, stirring occasionally, until translucent but not browned. Raise the heat to medium high, add the wine, and cook until slightly reduced, about 2 minutes. Transfer the leeks and butter-wine mixture to a blender and puree until smooth.

In a large bowl, toss together the leek puree, potatoes, cream, and cheese. Place the potato mixture in an 8- by 8-inch baking dish and cover with aluminum foil. Bake until tender, 1 to 1¼ hours, removing the foil the last 10 minutes to brown the top. Cut into squares and keep warm until ready to serve.

Heat a grill to medium, about 275°.

In a small bowl, combine the paprika, salt, and pepper. Rub the steaks thoroughly with the mixture and let rest for 5 minutes. Grill the steaks, 2 to 3 minutes on each side, flipping once, until medium rare. Remove from the grill and tent with foil.

In a large nonstick pan, melt the remaining tablespoon of butter over medium heat. Carefully crack the duck eggs into the pan and let cook until the yolks are soft but still runny, about 2 minutes, covering with a pan lid the final 30 seconds to thoroughly cook the whites. Top each steak with one egg and serve with a side of potatoes. Season with salt and pepper to taste and serve immediately.

Watercress, Crab, and Taleggio Salad with Honeycomb, Grapefruit, Marcona Almonds, and Pancetta Chips

Hal takes the basic flavor combinations in this salad—sweet, tart, and tangy—and varies them with the season. "Toss it in and see what comes out," he says. Fresh honeycomb is available at some farmers markets and specialty grocery stores.

Serves 8

1 large bunch (about 4 cups) watercress

Butter for baking sheet

8 pieces pancetta, thinly sliced in circles

½ cup (5 ounces) Marcona almonds

¼ cup 12-year-old sherry vinegar

¼ teaspoon kosher salt, plus additional

½ cup extra-virgin olive oil

¼ teaspoon freshly ground black pepper

8 ounces Taleggio (semisoft Italian cow's milk cheese), cubed

1 whole pink grapefruit, peeled, seeded, and sliced into 16 sections

8 ounces lump crabmeat, picked through

1 whole round honeycomb, chilled and sliced into 2- to 3-inch pieces

Preheat the oven to 350°. Cut the stems off the watercress and discard. Rinse the leaves and set aside on paper towels to dry.

Grease a baking sheet with butter. Lay the pancetta on the baking sheet, leaving 1 inch between each piece. Bake until crispy and starting to brown on the edges, about 5 minutes. Remove from the oven and set aside.

On a separate ungreased baking sheet, scatter the almonds and toast until lightly golden, stirring occasionally for about 4 to 6 minutes. Remove from the oven and set aside.

In a small bowl, combine the vinegar and a pinch of the salt. Slowly add the oil, whisking constantly, until emulsified. Add the remaining ¼ teaspoon salt and the pepper; mix well.

In a large bowl, combine the watercress and the vinaigrette, tossing lightly to combine. Divide among 8 serving plates and sprinkle with the almonds and cheese. Top each serving with 2 slices of grapefruit, a spoonful of crabmeat, 1 pancetta chip, and 1 slice of honeycomb. Season with salt and pepper to taste and serve immediately.

Cucumber Lime Cilantro Sorbet

You can churn this into a sorbet or freeze it in ice pop molds and serve as a palate cleanser. You'll need an electric juicer for the cucumber.

Makes 1¾ cups

> 1 cup water
>
> 1 cup sugar
>
> 2 tablespoons chopped cilantro
>
> 1 cucumber, freshly juiced (with an electric juicer)
>
> Juice of 3 limes

In a medium saucepan, bring the water and sugar to a boil. Add the cilantro, turn off the heat, and let sit on the stove for 3 minutes. Remove from the stove and set aside until cool.

Add the cucumber juice and lime juice; chill for 2 hours. Pour into ice pop molds and freeze for at least 6 hours or overnight. Or, freeze in an ice cream maker according to manufacturer's instructions. Spoon into a plastic container and freeze, covered, for at least 3 hours prior to serving.

Serve the ice pops directly from the molds or remove the sorbet from the freezer 10 minutes prior to serving and scoop into individual serving dishes.

OUTSTANDING
IN THE FIELD

Culinary celebrations at the source

Set between the soil and the sky, Outstanding in the Field's long, linen-draped table beckons adventurous diners to celebrate food at the source. Bringing together local farmers and food artisans, chefs and winemakers, we explore the connection between the earth and the food on your plate. Join us as we feast on the gifts of the land.

Outstanding in the Field events feature a leisurely tour of the hosting farm followed by a five-course, farm-style dinner at our long table set in a scenic spot. Dinner is accompanied by a wine paired with each course. Diners are joined at the table by the farmer, food producers, a winemaker and other local artisans associated with the meal.

—Outstanding in the Field

CHAPTER 9

"We have to stop at the drive-thru. I'm starving," says my husband, Kevin, as we pull out of the Coleman's driveway in Carpinteria.

Normally, I'd pull over at the first sight of french fries. But considering we've just paid $180 per person for a five-hour six-course dinner at Outstanding in the Field, a roving restaurant that orchestrates 130-person culinary events on farms, wineries, and other outdoor locations across the country, I'm not about to spend a couple of bucks on fast food. He'll have to go to bed hungry.

It's not that the food wasn't good. Rich Mead, executive chef at Sage and Sage on the Coast restaurants in nearby Newport Beach—and tonight's guest chef—prepared a farmers market-fresh Sunday night supper featuring locally sourced ingredients. The succotash was packed with just-picked corn and heirloom tomatoes, the braised beef short ribs were meltingly tender, and the cobbler was bursting with juicy peak-of-season grilled peaches. And the wines, all Rhone varietals including Viognier, Roussanne, and Picpoul Blanc grown in nearby Paso Robles by Tablas Creek Vineyard, were solid. But when dinner for two costs $360 or $400, depending on the night, you expect a full belly upon departure.

In 1999, when Jim Denevan, the forty-six-year-old former chef of Santa Cruz's Gabriella Café, founded Outstanding in the Field (known as OITF by staffers), he simply wanted to take people out of the restaurant and directly to the farm. "We were already doing farm fresh food at the restaurant and hosting special dinners with farmers," says Jim. "I wanted to take people further—to connect them to the land and the farmers so they would truly appreciate them."

Jim believes that farmers, not chefs, are the true artists of the culinary world. It's a heartfelt statement from a man who is both chef and artist. In his free time, Jim produces sand drawings to be captured in a fleeting snapshot then scattered away by the wind. And he understands those who provide for us: the farmers who quietly enrich our daily lives with fresh ingredients. Give individual farmers the recognition they deserve—the Thomas Keller of cranberry growers, the Nancy Silverton of legumes, the Mario Batali of green beans—and gradually the rest of the world will learn to appreciate them.

In the earliest years of OITF, Jim hosted two to three dinners on California farms during the summer while he continued to work at Gabriella. But in 2003 he quit his day job and hit the road. He bought a beat-up streamlined 1953 bus for $7,000, gathered a crew of volunteers and staff willing to work for spare change and the thrill of the culinary adventure, and headed

across North America during the summer of 2004. He was on a mission to change the way we experience food.

It was a dreamy—and refreshingly sincere—proposition.

OITF has never been a secretive, illusive affair: no lottery system tickets, no e-mails to prove your value as a coveted dinner guest, no friend-of-a-friend relationship required. Getting into an event is simply a matter of scrolling through the Web site, choosing a date and location, and submitting payment (all major credit cards accepted) before 120 other curious foodies do so first and the words *Sold Out* are plastered across the page.

Online event details are minimal. They offer the location and guest chef but little more. With fewer than fifteen OITF dinners throughout the summer and fall, choosing one is more a matter of drive time than seeking your ideal guest chef. More than half the dinners are in California; many of those are near the Santa Cruz area where Jim and several of his staff reside. The rest are scattered across the country in varying locations: Kinnikinnick Farm outside Chicago; La Plaza Cultural Community Garden in New York City; Smith-Berry Vineyard in New Castle, Kentucky; and University of British Columbia Farm in Vancouver.

For OITF, finding a suitable location depends on numerous factors: size (130 chairs take up quite a bit of space); location (remote enough to be quaint, but not too far that city dwellers capable of paying OITF prices won't make the drive); willingness of the farm, ranch, or winery to participate in an event; and whether the location is financially feasible and logistically possible.

I probably should have known by the motto on the e-mail signature line: *Celebrating Communities in Harmony with Nature.* Inviting a girlfriend to join me at tonight's dinner would have been a wise choice.

"You've got to be kidding me," my husband says, reading the OITF confirmation e-mail. "I just paid $180, and I'm supposed to bring my own plate? How is bringing my own plate about community? What's for dinner, anyway?"

I don't have any idea. OITF doesn't post menus in advance or give the slightest hint of what ingredients might be featured. Even a brief description of the chef's style—Italian, French, Japanese, or somewhere in between— would satisfy our curiosity.

Thanks to light traffic in Los Angeles, he won't have to wait long. We arrive an hour early and park in the middle of the dirt road as instructed by OITF signs.

"Are you sure we're in the right place?" asks Kevin, eyeing a few sheds, a ten-foot-tall scrap heap, and two portable toilets.

Click on photos of past dinners on OITF's Web site, and scenes of magazine-worthy dinner party spreads are unveiled: white tablecloth-covered tables snaking around hidden ravines and nestled among rolling hills, olive trees glistening in the sunset, a lone lamb munching on grape leaves amidst the vines.

A sixtyish man in jeans and a baseball cap is sitting on three tires stacked against the junk heap. He grins and stretches out an enormous, calloused hand. "I'm Bill," he says in between cigarette puffs. "Make yourself at home. The folks putting this thing on are around here somewhere.

I'm just the farmer." And he gets back to a conversation with the man sitting next to him.

We stand around for a few minutes, not sure what to do next. I know Bill and his son Romeo from the Santa Monica farmers market where I buy their gorgeous greens—hard-to-find leafy varieties such as *cavolo nero* (Tuscan kale), Treviso, and epazote. Bill is friendly but a man of precious few words, so I sense nothing more is coming.

Kevin and I decide to take a self-guided tour around the farm. Much of the property is dedicated to the two homes where three generations of Colemans live; the rest is speckled with small plots of greens and herbs wedged between chicken coops, trailers piled with rusty gear, and a falling-apart shed where a few crew workers are hanging out, smoking cigarettes. This is a true working farm, not some postcard-perfect image.

The Assumption of Risk of damage or injury is your responsibility at these events. We will encounter a variety of terrain and climatic conditions; a description of conditions and any preparatory recommendations will be detailed in the map mailer you will receive prior to the event. Please call with any further questions. Fun is what we intend these events to be: informational, adventurous, and delicious. We look forward to seeing you in the field.

—Outstanding in the Field

Tommy Oldre, a smiling blond in his late twenties, is sorting through this evening's selection of Tablas Creek wines at a small table in front of the junk heap. In keeping with the focus on local products, OITF events typically feature a nearby winery. For smaller wineries, dinners such as these are a chance to introduce their wines to an affluent audience. Judging by the $10 discount given to nondrinkers at OITF dinners, I suspect the wineries subsidize a good portion of their offerings—or at least offer a cut-rate price.

"So you're Tommy, the Tablas Creek winemaker?" I ask, reading the OITF invitation that says that the winemaker will be attending.

"No, I wish! I'm Tommy, but I'm just a sales guy," he says, shoving a box of 2006 rosé underneath the table. He's driven to Carpinteria after a whirlwind week of trade tastings and high-end dinners at Los Angeles–area restaurants. OITF is his last stop before heading home to Paso Robles for a few days of downtime.

I leave Kevin to chat about Paso wines with Tommy while I look for Jim.

Around the corner behind a small patch of trees sits the other half of the farm—the half we missed. It could be straight from one of those perfect photos: nestled among rolling hills on one side, mountains on the other, and a handful of horses roaming in the corral below are two rows of pristine white tablecloth-covered banquet tables speckled with pink peony-filled clay pots.

Jim is easy to spot. He looks exactly the same as in every glossy magazine feature: signature straw cowboy hat pulled low on his weather-beaten face, button-down shirt with the sleeves rolled up, pressed jeans, foam flip-flops—and a camera crew in tow.

Katy Oursler, OITF director-coordinator-organizer extraordinaire, is doling out instructions to the half-dozen assistants lined up around the banquet tables. She's been involved with OITF since the early days. When she heard about Jim's vision and philosophy, she attended a dinner and fell in love with the idea. With the help of two paid assistants and a handful of volunteers, Katy handles all OITF logistics—answering thousands of e-mails from past, current, and potential customers; arranging portable toilet deliveries (and making sure the lovely bud vase filled with fresh flowers is strategically placed on a tiny side table between them); dealing with press inquiries; and, most recently, blogging about past dinners. Without Katy OITF dinners wouldn't happen, Jim says. He's too much of a free spirit to deal with such details. It's a perfect balance.

"Make sure those chairs are solid on the hilly end!" she yells to an assistant on the opposite end of the table. "It's 3:45. Are we all set out front?"

Rich tosses sliced ciabatta onto the grill. He and a handful of line cooks from the restaurant have been here since noon, shucking corn for the succotash, chopping tomatoes for the bruschetta, and grilling peaches for the

cobbler. Most of tonight's menu features fresh produce requiring last-minute on-site prep. A few dishes, like the slow-cooked short ribs, were brought over from the restaurant to manage the time—and oven—constraints of cooking in a mobile kitchen. Rich has a decent-sized kitchen with a four-foot grill, a single oven with an eight-burner range, and two prep tables. But one oven doesn't do much when you're talking about 130 hungry diners.

"Did you taste the cantaloupe I brought?" Alex Weiser asks as he hands me a slice. I've seen Alex, purveyor of Weiser Family Farms, every Wednesday at the Santa Monica market for years, although we've never formally met. "I'd never heard of these kinds of farm dinners, had you? It sounded pretty cool, so I figured I'd come hang out and check it out, bring some potatoes and things," he says, slicing up more melons for the crew.

My husband is still standing where I left him, chatting with Tommy over a glass of wine. At 4:00 sharp, Katy appears at the front entrance of the farm, freshly dressed in a pink-striped knit sundress, her hair knotted into two loose buns. She stations herself between two rusty wheelbarrows, smoothes her dress, and scans the wine table to make sure Tommy has everything in order. "Jim, where are you?" she yells. Jim appears from around the corner, with the camera crew right behind him.

The first guests are already wandering up the dirt road; others are looking for a place to park their SUVs. The crowd is a varied age range—midtwenties to late sixties—but judging by the Hermès handbags, Pucci sundresses, and Italian loafers, not a particularly diverse socioeconomic slice of Southern California.

"Oh, yes, I see your name here as paid," says Katy with a smile. "And you decided to bring your friend after all? I'm sure we can find the room to squeeze her in. Did you want to go ahead and write a check to settle up?"

Most guests have brought a plate as instructed. Katy instructs them to set them in the wheelbarrow on her right; the other wheelbarrow is meant for jackets and scarves that won't be needed until the cool breeze rolls in later this evening. Several women reluctantly hold on to their wraps, clearly not willing to put their delicate cashmere cardigans into a rusty wheelbarrow.

"You'd be surprised; sometimes we've even had private limos drive up and drop people off," Jim says as he saunters away after he greets the last guest.

"I feel like we're at a wedding and we don't know anyone except the bride and groom," Kevin whispers, empty wineglass in hand. Judging by hugs, many of the guests are friends who have met here. Others appear to be multigenerational families, with Mom and Dad. Most are couples; single diners are noticeably lacking.

An assistant places a platter of tomato bruschetta on a small table next to Tommy. No one touches it. Maybe they're saving room for dinner or worried about fitting into that Academy Awards dress—so Kevin and I dive right in. It's good, a homey Italian-style appetizer topped with diced heirloom tomatoes, fresh herbs, and a drizzle of olive oil.

"Tastes like that bruschetta you made the other night," says Kevin, which I take as a compliment.

Tommy is sweating even though it's cooled off ten degrees in the past hour. It's a few minutes before 5:00 and the cocktail hour shows no sign of waning. He's running out of rosé, the same wine he's serving for the first course, so he's been forced to pour a shallow three ounces per glass, standard at winery-sponsored events but not exactly what OITF dinner guests have in mind.

"The natives are restless; let's get a move on it," Tommy says out the side of his mouth to Kevin. "If they'd told me cocktail hour would literally be an hour, I'd have brought more wine. And this looks like more than one hundred people."

In the kitchen Rich is getting a bit restless, too. He'd planned on serving the first course at 5:15 but the farm tour hasn't even begun. He's worried about the steamed sea bass. It can't sit out much longer at room temperature, but if he steams it now, it will be mushy when he reheats it.

"Something is going to have to give," he says half to himself, half to his crew, just as Jim and Katy gather the guests together for a group welcome.

"It's rare you get to see into a kitchen, gather around a table with so many people, and share a farmer-grown meal, right here on the farm with the actual farmers and chefs," says Katy.

It's a feel-good moment and the guests love it, hands clasped at their chests ready to break into applause at any moment. Jim stands up to give a short speech about the OITF mission and to introduce Bill Coleman and his farm. But it's clearly Jim who is the star tonight—the gorgeous, sun-drenched cowboy chef—and the celebrity chef du jour. He receives a barrage of questions: why he started OITF, how he maneuvers each dinner, his personal cooking style.

The farm tour finally dispatches, not to return until almost 6:00. Katy announces that dinner is officially ready by clanking a large bell. She'll ring it throughout the evening anytime she wants our attention.

We're told to find our plates, which have been stacked on a table in the corner, before grabbing a seat. For those without a plate, like Kevin, a stash of plates is available in the corner. He's at the "extra" plate station and looks a bit uncomfortable. Other than the farmers and two latecomers, pretty much everyone else is in the "brought a plate" line.

Maybe it's something about a ringing bell, but suddenly this well-heeled bunch turns into a swarm of middle schoolers scrambling for the best seat on the bus.

"Get my plate!" yells one man in his late thirties as he trots to the end of a table to claim a seat for his wife and their friends. He's not alone in his "I called it first" table tactics, leaving the rest of us—individual couples—to fill in among the larger groups.

Kevin manages to score the head of one table—mainly because it required the longest walk. By the time I arrive, a lovely looking couple in their midsixties is sitting to his left. On my right is a couple in their late

thirties from Los Angeles and a group from Santa Barbara (whom we'll never meet).

At each place is a computer-printed menu with a special thanks to the purveyors of tonight's ingredients. In addition to Rich Mead and crew from Sage Restaurant and Tablas Creek Winery, the list includes a half-dozen local farms, dairies, and meat purveyors, and an artisan olive oil producer.

The first course, platters of Thai-style raw vegetable lettuce wraps, arrives within minutes. Rich has been waiting more than an hour to get those out of the kitchen, and Tommy needs to switch wines because he's out of the first course pairing. The wraps taste exactly like they sound—minced raw vegetables wrapped in lettuce with a hint of a spicy-sweet sauce. Refreshing, but definitely not screaming for seconds (not that there are any). Serving 130 people in a makeshift kitchen isn't exactly fodder for culinary nirvana.

Katy rings her bell. "We wanted to tell you a little more about the tradition of the plates because it's a question we inevitably get at every dinner. A farmer who came to a dinner told us to stop using the word *catering* to describe our events because this is so different, so unique. He suggested we ask guests to bring their own plates so it's clear how far this experience is from a typical catered dinner."

There is a pause as the guests absorb her statement. "Oh, and a lot of plates break when you travel eight thousand miles!" Katy adds with a laugh. She sits back down and we all get back to dinner.

The older couple beside us is charming. "We've come to OITF to experience something new. We read about it in a magazine or somewhere, and it sounded like an adventure," the wife says.

We talk about the couple's son and grandchildren, and about life in general, while the man on our right expounds on his extensive knowledge of wine and his wine cellar with its coveted, high-dollar contents.

Tommy fills our glasses with a 2005 Esprit de Beaucastel blanc, a crisp, spicy white, for the much anticipated steamed local sea bass and baby vegetables. He's clearly relieved, the Code Red rosé shortage behind him.

Before each course is served, Jim and Katy, along with their staff, line up with platters of food. When Katy gives the signal, they parade to the tables in unison with ear-to-ear smiles (it's all being captured on film). It's an oddly formal food presentation for such a community-driven event.

The food at OITF is served family style, a perfectly charming idea meant to instill a sense of community and encourage us to talk to our tablemates. But the Santa Barbara group has no desire to sully its comfortable conversation with small talk. The platters, although meant to generously serve four or five, offer only nibbles. And one of the Santa Barbara women is serving herself from our platter while the rest of her threesome are sharing one platter among themselves. The bell rings again and Phil McGrath of McGrath Family Farms stands up to talk about baby beans and haricots verts. He grows several fruits and vegetables on his nearby farm in Camarillo. "If I have a claim to fame, it would be lima beans," he says, chuckling.

All hundred-plus pairs of eyes are focused on him, and Phil isn't sure what to say next. Katy prods him with questions, asking him to tell us what his farm is like, his guiding principles, the reason he chose to be a farmer. She'd be a good television news host.

Tonight is an opportunity for the guests to get to know the farmers, but it doesn't seem to be working out that way. The farmers have congregated at one end of the table, likely because those were the only seats available.

"Trouble on the grill," says Rich, pulling off the Italian sausages that will accompany the short ribs for the next course. Alex is standing next to him, poking at a sausage. The grill didn't get hot enough and they're undercooked, but the plates need to go out in the next five minutes.

"See if any of them turned out and let's slice those up," Rich instructs one of the line cooks. "Get rid of the rest."

I have a couple of potato questions for Alex, who's known as the potato king of the SoCal farming world. The Santa Monica farmers market is always too packed to get any kind of real conversation going; it's like a "hockey game" of produce buyers, as Alex calls it. In the lull of tonight's dinner, he's more than happy to oblige in a little potato chat.

"Uh, Miss, I'm gonna be coming through right where you're standing in about two minutes, so you'll need to move," the cameraman informs me. "Just need the farmers and staff for this next shot."

And that's that. So much for chatting with my local potato farmer at a farm dinner.

At our table the conversation has turned to food: a not-to-miss taco stand in Hermosa Beach, a local artisan vinegar producer, the best potted pear trees at the Santa Barbara market.

"The one I bought last year has been to hell and back with the weather, but it's still turning out really good pears," says the lovely retiree across from us.

Platters of braised short ribs and grilled sausage are paraded in front of the camera and land on the table in front of us, along with a heaping bowl of succotash made from Alex's heirloom carrots and corn. The succotash is amazing, speckled with sweet heirloom tomatoes and fresh herbs—the best dish we've had all night. And it's in a huge bowl, more than enough for everyone. The men look pleased.

My husband looks at the short rib and sausage platter longingly as it makes the rounds. But by the time it gets back to him, only a tiny two-inch nub of short rib remains. He scoops it up along with several thin slices of the sausage.

"Mine's raw in the middle," he whispers.

Kevin hasn't had more than ten bites from the four courses, but he's happy because he's befriended Tommy, who gives him a generous pour of wine each time he appears.

"Hey, how'd you swing a full glass of wine?" asks the cellar snob when he eyes Kevin's syrah.

Jim, Katy, and their two paid full-time assistants camped out last night on the Coleman Farms property and will do so again this evening. It's one way they keep costs down—no motel rentals. But there's more to it than that. They enjoy spending the evening before a big event with the farmers over an intimate, casual supper—nothing fancy or expensive, just a group of folks hanging out and getting to know one another—their hopes, dreams, and aspirations.

Veronica is the assistant who handles OITF customer phone calls. She had attended a fund-raiser Outstanding in the Field hosted for a nonprofit insurance company in Santa Cruz, the organization where she works. "After that, I was totally sold," she says. "I've done every dinner since. I used to take the time off work and volunteer for OITF, although this year they're actually paying us a little, which is nice, so I've taken a full leave of absence to go on tour with them. It's so much fun!"

Back at the table, the last of the succotash has been passed around.

"I love it when the wind shifts and you know you're on a farm because of the distinct smell of pig manure," says the wine snob next to us. It's nearing 8:00, with only the cheese and dessert courses to come. I mention to Kevin that we should be back home by 10:00, depending on traffic.

"You mean you're not staying at one of the fabulous hotels in Santa Barbara? There are so many there to choose from," says the wine snob's girlfriend.

Uh, well, we're driving home for the same reason Jim and Katy and crew camp out on the farms they visit. It's free.

The dinner plates have been collected and are being furiously hand washed in time for the guests' departure. Rich is slicing two enormous wheels of Rinconada Dairy Pozo Tomme and placing the slices on individual dessert plates for the cheese course.

"This is the biggest piece of anything we've been served so far," says a guy at the table next to us. We've heard hardly a peep of the other table's conversation—or from anyone other than the six people sitting around us—until now. "Too bad it's awful with the wine."

His girlfriend nudges him. "I think everything has been perfect—it's just so amazing to be here. I mean, where else can you get this?" she says.

She's right. I've never had an experience quite like this. It was a lovely evening, and truly unique. But I just can't get past the price. No doubt it's expensive to put on these events, but $180 to $200 a person? It had better be perfect.

It's gotten cool—some people are searching for their sweaters in the wheelbarrow. A couple of bats are flying overhead looking for their own dinner. Plenty of mosquitoes are down below for them, and us, to enjoy.

The grilled peach cobbler drizzled with a crème fraîche and vanilla bean honey sauce is excellent, so good I'm tempted to lick the bowl. I polish off my cobbler and head to the mobile kitchen where I figure I can talk my way into an extra helping. Rich is only too happy to oblige.

"We're about at the point when we can kick back and have a drink," he says, grinning. "I've done a lot of catering, but this one was hard because I wasn't in charge of everything, or really anything. I just showed up with my staff. You never know what will happen."

Considering his constraints, Rich turned out an impressive menu. All the more reason I can't wait to have dinner at Sage Restaurant . . . on his turf.

As if on cue, a rainbow pops up over the mountains. It's picture perfect (as long as you take the photo just to the left of the cameramen heatedly discussing what time they can leave).

We say our goodbyes as the crew heaps large bowls of succotash, short ribs, and cobbler onto serving trays for the staff meal. Jim personally thanks departing guests, shaking their hands as they leave. It was a lovely evening, and I don't doubt that Jim and Katy are completely genuine in their quest to help American farmers. But it's hard not to notice that OITF has become a pricey playground.

We have a long drive home, so Kevin and I head toward our car, giving Tommy, Rich, and Alex hugs along the way. As we leave Jim says sotto voce, perhaps sensing our disappointment, "You know, tonight really was a little unusual. It seemed like a very L.A. crowd."

I can't help but wonder exactly what he means by an "L.A. crowd." Affluent?

"Too bad we don't have kids," Kevin says as he pulls the car door shut. "They would have gotten $10 off for not drinking wine."

RECIPES

Heirloom Tomato Bruschetta with Garlic Butter, Fresh Mozzarella, and Arugula

Sage Executive Chef Rich Mead insists it's a must to make this simple appetizer with peak-of-the-season, flavorful heirloom tomatoes. Leftover garlic butter will keep, refrigerated, for 1 week.

Serves 6

1 stick (½ cup) butter, at room temperature

2 cloves garlic, minced

1 tablespoon grated Parmigiano-Reggiano cheese

2 teaspoons chopped parsley

2 medium heirloom tomatoes

1 8-ounce ball fresh mozzarella

6 slices country bread or other rustic European-style bread

1 bunch arugula leaves, washed and dried

Kosher salt

Freshly ground black pepper

Extra-virgin olive oil for drizzling

Preheat the grill or broiler to medium high.

In a small bowl, combine the butter, garlic, Parmigiano-Reggiano, and parsley. Set aside.

With a sharp knife, cut each tomato horizontally into 6 slices. Cut the mozzarella horizontally into 6 slices.

Spread 2 teaspoons of the garlic butter on 1 side of each bread slice. Grill or broil until the bread begins to brown on the edges, about 5 minutes. Transfer to a large serving platter and place 2 to 3 arugula leaves on each bread slice and top with 2 tomato slices. Sprinkle with the salt and pepper, top with 1 slice of mozzarella, and drizzle with the oil. Serve immediately.

Rich's Heirloom Cherry Tomato Jam

At the restaurant Rich serves this tangy tomato jam with just about anything he can find: seafood, fish, and crusty bread. Or stir a few tablespoons together with pasta, good-quality olive oil, and Parmigiano-Reggiano.

2 tablespoons extra-virgin olive oil

1 cup minced red onion

2 cloves garlic, minced

3 pints heirloom cherry tomatoes

1 4-inch sprig rosemary

1 sprig thyme

Kosher salt

Freshly ground black pepper

In a medium saucepan, heat the oil over medium heat. Add the onion and cook until translucent but not browned. Add the garlic and sauté for 1 minute. Increase the heat to medium high and add the tomatoes, rosemary, and thyme. Cook, stirring occasionally, until tomatoes burst, about 10 minutes. Remove from the heat and season with the salt and pepper. Cover and refrigerate for up to 1 week. Serve at room temperature.

Grilled Peach Cobbler
with Vanilla Crème Fraîche

This is a simple, easy-to-make dish. Rich recommends experimenting with various peaches, depending on what's in season at your farmers market. After dinner invite your guests to help you grill the peaches. Be sure to allow at least 2 hours to chill and bake the crumble.

Serves 6

¼ cup honey

1 teaspoon ground cinnamon

½ vanilla bean, scraped (reserve other ½ for Vanilla Crème Fraîche)

3 large peaches, halved and pitted

Crumble (recipe follows)

Vanilla Crème Fraîche (recipe follows)

In a medium bowl, combine the honey, cinnamon, and vanilla bean. Add the peaches and marinate for 1 hour or up to 3 hours.

Preheat the grill or broiler to high. Reserving the marinade, remove peaches from the marinade and grill until soft but not falling apart, about 3 minutes. Set aside.

In a medium saucepan, bring the marinade to a boil. Reduce to a simmer and cook until reduced by half, about 6 to 8 minutes. Set aside.

To assemble, place 1 grilled peach half on each plate and drizzle with the marinade. Sprinkle with 2 tablespoons of the crumble and 1 tablespoon of the crème fraîche. Serve immediately.

Crumble

1¾ cups all-purpose flour

1 teaspoon kosher salt

1 tablespoon sugar

1 tablespoon baking powder

6 tablespoons cold butter

¾ cup heavy cream

In a medium bowl, combine the flour, salt, sugar, and baking powder. Cut in the butter until the mixture resembles coarse meal. Add the cream and mix until the crumble just comes together. Chill for 1 hour.

Preheat the oven to 325°. Roll out the crumble dough to ½ inch thick. Transfer to a baking sheet and bake until golden brown, about 20 to 25 minutes. Cool and crumble with your hands.

Vanilla Crème Fraîche

1 cup crème fraîche

¼ cup honey

½ vanilla bean, scraped (other ½ used for Grilled Peaches)

1 teaspoon vanilla extract

1 tablespoon lemon zest

In a small bowl, combine all the ingredients. Refrigerate for up to 3 days until ready to serve.

FARMERS MARKET WEDNESDAYS

~

FARMERS MARKET WEDNESDAYS

ON SUNDAY

Reunion dinner, September 16, 8 PM

Roasted Figs with Prosciutto, Gorgonzola & Aged Balsamic

Heirloom Tomato & Burrata Tart with Basil Oil

Pan-Roasted Monkfish with Fresh Shelling Beans,
Sautéed Bitter Greens and Saffron Aioli

Last of Summer Peach Crumble with Crème Fraîche Ice Cream

What to bring: A thoughtful bottle of wine

All ingredients come from suppliers practicing sustainable agriculture

~

CHAPTER 10

"Come on, tell her the truth," says Josh Loeb, thirty-two, and owner of Rustic Canyon Wine Bar and Seasonal Kitchen in Santa Monica. "All I did was watch."

Zoe Nathan, Rustic Canyon's bubbly twentysomething pastry chef, gives Josh a play-along-with-it glance as she pops a tub of crème fraîche ice cream into the freezer. "No, really, he made them," she says to me, pointing at the individual ramekins of brown-butter peach crumble on the kitchen counter.

But the telltale restaurant-grade heavy-duty plastic wrap gives her away.

"OK. Maybe he just helped," she relents, twirling around Josh's one-hundred-square-foot kitchen. "But he helped a lot."

"Yeah, I passed by the pastry station and stuck my finger in them," Josh says, smiling.

Tonight, Kevin and I are guests at Farmers Market Wednesdays, the underground restaurant Josh held in his parents' Rustic Canyon home and later in his Los Angeles apartment for four years. "Are you going to keep this underground thing going?" a guest asks Josh.

"Well, now that the restaurant is going I don't have much time," says Josh, stuffing fresh figs with Gorgonzola cheese. "But I kind of miss it, actually. The restaurant is very different. Maybe I'll try to fit in a dinner every once in a while. You all are going to have to remind me!"

We're here with a dozen guests to find out what happens when a "successful" underground restaurant becomes a legit brick-and-mortar operation. Tonight is the first Farmers Market Wednesdays Josh has held since his restaurant opened eight months ago. Usually, guests are culled from a mailing list of more than 150 friends, friends of friends, and strangers. But tonight, all the invitees are friends or Rustic Canyon employees.

"This is more a reunion of sorts," he says. "I used to send out invites to the mailing list and just let whoever replied come, but now that I've got the restaurant, I might as well invite who I want, right?"

"When Josh told us six years ago he was thinking about opening a restaurant, we thought he was crazy," says Daina Danovitch, a physician and wife of his childhood friend Itai. They've arrived early to help with the final preparations for tonight's dinner. "We didn't have any idea he was so into cooking. It came out of nowhere."

Josh worked as a copy editor in Manhattan after college, but the quiet, introspective work didn't suit him. He got the itch to open a restaurant while "sitting in restaurants and coffee shops watching the owners interact with customers . . . I wanted to be that person," he says, smoothing his curly black hair. "Only I didn't really know how to run a restaurant."

For four years prior to opening Rustic Canyon, Josh floated around various restaurant jobs, first as a waiter at a local deli and eventually working his way up to wine manager at Capo, Bruce Marder's high-end Italian bistro in Santa Monica.

"I wanted feedback on the food I was cooking, to see what people liked and didn't like . . . and Farmers Market Wednesdays seemed like the best way to do that," he says, methodically wrapping paper-thin slices of prosciutto around the Gorgonzola-stuffed figs. "Not that I'm a really great cook."

He named the underground dinners after the Santa Monica farmers market held each Wednesday where he shopped for produce: pumpkin squash, pomegranates, and artisan cheeses one week; grass-fed bison, purple Peruvian potatoes, and broccoli rabe the next. At home he cooked three-course family-style meals for the twelve to fourteen guests. A typical menu might include grilled calamari with lemon aioli and tomatillo salsa, butternut squash risotto with fried zucchini blossoms, and home-made doughnuts with Vahlrona hot chocolate. Not bad for a guy who says he doesn't cook.

In the beginning guests paid $10 and brought a "thoughtful bottle of wine" to pair with the food. But as word got out, the e-mail list swelled to more than 100 people, the monthly gatherings turned into weekly affairs, and Josh raised the price to $20, just enough to help cover expenses and keep the dinners going.

"At some point they stopped being dinners with my friends and turned into gatherings with a houseful of people I didn't know," he says. "People would e-mail me asking if I was holding a dinner that Wednesday and could they get a spot. It was great."

But Josh wanted to open a restaurant, a real restaurant. "I wanted a true neighborhood bistro, the kind of place people gather for a glass of wine and a shared plate, not just another of those L.A. restaurants with fussy food at crazy prices. It took longer and was much harder than I thought."

In early fall 2006, four years after his first underground dinner, Josh drove past a boarded-up Chinese restaurant in a Santa Monica strip mall with a For Lease sign out front—not exactly his dream space but a good location with affordable rent. And with years of hosting underground dinners, testing recipes, and entertaining strangers, he knew exactly the type of food to serve and the atmosphere he wanted to create.

Chris, a television producer and Zoe's new beau, plops down an armload of supplies he's carted from the restaurant. "Oh, fantastic!" says Zoe, grabbing half a stack of cloth towels and handing the rest to Samir Mohajer, thirty-one, Rustic Canyon's executive chef. "I'm dying without real towels." Paper towels and professional chefs don't mix well.

"Hey Josh, where's your cinnamon?" Zoe asks, peering into the half-empty kitchen cupboards. She's wedged between Samir and a sheet pan of pastries teetering atop tubs of food prepped at the restaurant. Josh moved into the house a few months ago, shortly after the restaurant opened, and hasn't had time to fully settle in. "And do you have any, like,

nuts or anything around here? I should have told Chris to bring more stuff from the restaurant."

Daina and Itai are carefully lining up square white plates and sturdy flatware on the long wood table in the living room, just as they did when Josh hosted his underground events. Like the restaurant, the space is sparse but warmly decorated with simple wood furniture. Josh surveys the room to make sure everything is in order. He planned the menu tonight, but the figs are the only part of tonight's dinner he's preparing.

"Now that I have a professional chef and pastry chef on staff, I'd be crazy to cook," he says, pulling the figs off the grill. "And besides, I'm not a chef, right?"

Jon Hoeber, a screenwriter with a penchant for cocktails, arrives with two liquor bottles filled with lime-green liquid tucked under his arm. He tosses his leather bomber jacket on the chair and gets to work, no introductions required. The other guests, a mix of Josh's friends and restaurant employees, all appear to know him.

"It's a basil martini," he says, scanning the dining room for cocktail glasses. Josh doesn't have any martini glasses, so he settles for champagne flutes. "Pureed basil, fresh lime juice, vodka, and a little simple syrup. Getting just the right amount of lime juice is the key."

Jon designed Rustic Canyon's cocktail menu, a selection of drinks using Prosecco rather than spirits, because the restaurant has only a beer and wine license. He got the gig as "consulting mixologist" (fancy name for a friend who kindly helps out behind the bar) after he attended a

Farmers Market Wednesdays dinner and brought along a few jars of his unique infusions.

"I met several people for the restaurant through my underground dinners," says Josh. "Jon for cocktails and a couple of investors in the restaurant."

The seasonal cocktail menu includes the Kumquat Sunrise (muddled kumquats, ruby port, and Prosecco), the Black and Blue (freshly pressed blackberry juice, Prosecco, blueberry garnish), and Indochine (lemongrass- and ginger-infused simple syrup and Prosecco).

"You'd better grab one now because when they're gone, they're gone," Josh instructs us, handing over a large platter loaded with grilled figs oozing with melted Gorgonzola and finished with a drizzle of eighteen-year-old balsamic vinegar.

Jon pops one in his mouth as he heads toward the door, leather jacket in hand. "Good stuff. Back in a bit—I forgot the limoncello I made a while back. Thought we'd have it after dessert."

"Samir, come on, sit down with us," says Josh as we stand around the table in anticipation of the first course.

"Later," says the chef, completely focused on the monkfish he's sautéing. The rest of us grab a chair around the dining table.

"I want to thank all of you for coming," says Josh. "Many of you have been coming to Farmers Market Wednesdays since the beginning. Tonight is a celebration of how far we've come. But I guess since tonight is Sunday, we should change the name." Sunday is the only night the restaurant is closed and the only night Josh can host the occasional dinner, especially when his staff is doing the cooking.

Stacie Livingston, the restaurant's day manager, and Zoë serve the heirloom tomato and burrata cheese tart drizzled with basil oil. They take a seat at the table, a rare opportunity to sit and enjoy a meal they prepared.

Josh has uncorked the wine the guests brought and has placed them on the dining table. At most BYOB underground restaurants, such as HUSH in Washington, D.C., the bring-your-own wine isn't usually shared. Here, it is expected. When you're charging only $20, everyone is more of a guest than an outright customer, happy to share their food . . . and their wine.

Josh instructs all the guests to introduce their bottles by offering a story about the wine—either fact or fiction.

"Since this is a very special dinner, I wanted to share a wine I brought back from a recent visit to Tuscany," says Linda, a health care statistical analyst. At the first few underground dinners she helped Josh with the shopping and cooking. Now she's an investor in the restaurant. "Earlier today I was reflecting on one of the first dinners when we made homemade pappardelle pasta, so tonight seemed like a good time to open something nice—and Italian—to celebrate Josh's success."

"Come on, you got it from the wineshop on your way over," says Josh, grinning. "Let's eat."

The tart is fantastic—oozing with burrata, a three-day-old mozzarella stuffed with fresh curd and cream, and slathered with homemade tomato sauce. When all the plates are wiped clean, Stacie instinctively jumps up to ask if anyone would like seconds and refills our water glasses with a smile, a day manager even on her day off.

"In the first few months we struggled to find the right people, especially with waitstaff," says Josh. "I didn't want a rotating crew of actor-waiter types or disinterested kitchen staff. The people who work here needed to believe in the concept, and that can be difficult to find. For Farmers Market Wednesdays it didn't matter so much—it was so laid back so I just took care of everything. But people expect a lot more in a restaurant."

Choosing the right chef was the most pressing problem. He wanted the restaurant's cuisine to reflect a style similar to his own. But he knew he couldn't simply re-create home recipes on a larger scale.

"One of my favorite desserts I did for Farmers Market Wednesdays was a white chocolate soup speckled with semifrozen blueberries. But it would never work at the restaurant because you can't anticipate when a dessert order will be up. The berries would be too frozen or thawed completely and then it's just a bunch of rock hard or mushy blueberries floating in a sweet chocolate soup. Not good."

A friend recommended Samir, an Iranian-born chef who was working as a line cook at a French-Moroccan restaurant in Los Angeles. "We sat down and chatted, I cooked for him, and that was it," recalls Samir. "If Josh likes you, he trusts you."

Clearly, it was a good match. Samir's California-Mediterranean comfort food is remarkably similar to Josh's underground fare, albeit with a Moroccan flair: fingerling potato, caramelized onion, and feta *pizetta*; pan-roasted jidori chicken with bitter greens and pan jus; pork osso buco with potato confit.

"This wine is very special to me," says Chris, standing to announce his wine. "It's made with a new grape varietal from Harlem that's very difficult to find . . . and fermented with young mozzarella. The grapes were stomped by Clinton, so you'll notice the faint taste of his feet in the wine. I think you're going to really like it."

Stacie and Josh bring out large family-style platters of pan-roasted monkfish with fresh shelling beans, sautéed bitter greens, and saffron aioli.

At the restaurant, Josh has tried to preserve the communal aspect of the underground dinners by offering large portions to encourage diners to share. "I wanted to create an atmosphere where you could linger over dinner, sit down at the communal dining tables, and hang out with people you don't know. The kind of place you don't want to leave, like the way it was at Farmers Market Wednesdays." To encourage customer interaction, Rustic Canyon has three large communal dining tables in the middle of the room. But in a formal restaurant environment, sharing a table with other dinner guests isn't always as much fun as it is at an underground restaurant. Three months after opening, when one Los Angeles restaurant critic berated the communal tables, Josh decided two of them had to be sent to the chopping block.

I'm extremely thankful that, over the course of three visits, I never ended up at one of the communal tables, which occupy the majority of the room. I simply loathe communal dining . . . And, yes, I've read on the restaurant's Web site that this place was inspired by various dinner parties at the owner's house, where there was always a new face at the table. But . . . we're talking about the wildly divergent possibilities of guests at a very public restaurant. It's not always free love and camaraderie. This isn't Chez Panisse in the '60s. Sit with a bunch of strangers? At the airport, maybe. But here? No thanks.

—*Angeleno* magazine, July 2007

"This chef is really good," whispers Kevin, as we polish off the monkfish.

I wipe up the last of the saffron aioli with the monkfish just as Samir slips outside to smoke a cigarette. For him, this is just another night's work. He reappears and slumps on the sofa with a glass of wine. Josh opens several bottles of port brought by the guests, and Jon passes around his homemade limoncello.

"Well, the ice cream is a little hard," announces Josh as he sets a warm ceramic dish bubbling with buttery peaches in front of each couple. "So we're just going to scoop it onto the crumble as it thaws."

"I usually don't get to sit and eat dinner, so I completely forgot about dessert!" says Zoe, blushing. She brings the plastic tub of crème fraîche ice cream to the table and uses her body weight to dig into the ice cream. She pulls up on the scooper and a chunk flies across the room. "You can pick it up off the floor, we're not at the restaurant! Just kidding."

"I'm going to keep one of the communals. I just can't get rid of it. And I'm convinced that some people really do like it," Josh says, between bites of crumble.

Spreading the love is a bit harder at a restaurant.

Postscript: One year after he opened Rustic Canyon, Josh chopped up the last communal table.

RECIPES

Jon's Basil Martini

The cocktail base can be made several hours ahead, covered, and refrigerated.

Makes 12 cocktails

4 cups vodka

2 cups fresh basil leaves, loosely packed

½ cup freshly squeezed lime juice

¼ cup simple syrup (recipe follows)

¾ cup water

12 firm cherry tomatoes Ice

Place 12 small martini glasses in the freezer to chill.

In a blender combine the vodka and basil. Puree until smooth. Add the lime juice, simple syrup, and water, and pulse until thoroughly combined. Strain the mixture through a fine-mesh sieve and refrigerate until ready to use.

Pour 6 ounces of the vodka mixture into a cocktail shaker. Fill with ice, cover, and shake until chilled. Strain into a chilled martini glass. Serve immediately.

Simple Syrup

Makes about ¾ cup

½ cup sugar

½ cup water

In a medium saucepan, combine the sugar and water and cook over medium heat until the sugar is dissolved, about 5 minutes. Cover and refrigerate for up to 2 months.

Grilled Figs with Prosciutto and Aged Balsamic

Serves 12

24 firm Genoa or Black Mission figs, stems removed

8 ounces Gorgonzola cheese, cut into 24 cubes

24 thin slices Prosciutto di Parma

2 tablespoons olive oil

2 tablespoons 12- to 18-year-old balsamic vinegar

Kosher salt

Preheat the grill to high or the oven to 450°.

Rinse the figs and pat dry. With a paring knife cut a small slit in the bottom of each fig. Insert a cube of cheese and with your fingers gently squeeze the opening closed. Wrap 1 slice of prosciutto around each fig, rolling the fig to blanket it completely. Repeat with the remaining figs and place on the grill. With the lid closed, grill until the figs are browned on 1 side, about 4 minutes. Flip the figs and repeat.

Alternatively, preheat the broiler to high and place the figs in a roasting pan. Broil until browned, about 2 minutes. Flip the figs and broil another 2 minutes or until golden brown and soft.

Place the warm figs on a serving platter and drizzle with the oil and vinegar. Sprinkle with the salt to taste. Serve immediately.

Pan-Roasted Monkfish with Sautéed Bitter Greens and Saffron Aioli

The monkfish recipe can easily be doubled to serve 12, but use 2 pans to avoid overcrowding. You will have plenty of aioli.

Serves 6

6 6-ounce medallions monkfish

½ teaspoon kosher salt, plus additional

¼ teaspoon white pepper, plus additional

¼ cup canola oil

3 tablespoons extra-virgin olive oil

¼ cup minced shallots

1 teaspoon crushed red chile flakes

4 bunches dandelion greens, cut into 2-inch pieces

Saffron Aioli (recipe follows)

Preheat the oven to 400°.

Season both sides of the monkfish with the salt and pepper. Set aside.

In a large sauté pan, heat the canola oil until smoking. Sear the fish until golden brown on 1 side, about 2 minutes. Flip the fish and repeat. Bake until the fish flakes but is still juicy, about 8 to10 minutes.

Meanwhile, in a large sauté pan heat the olive oil over medium high heat. Add the shallots and chile flakes and cook for 30 seconds. Add the dandelion greens and continue cooking until wilted, about 3 minutes. Season with the salt and pepper to taste.

Plate the dandelion greens on a large serving platter. Arrange the monkfish on top and finish with a dollop of saffron aioli on each piece of fish. Serve immediately.

Saffron Aioli

The aioli can be made up to 1 day ahead, covered, and refrigerated. Leftover aioli is great as a vegetable dip, spread onto a sandwich like mayonnaise, or thinned with a little red wine vinegar to make salad dressing.

Makes 1½ cups (12 servings with monkfish or 6 with leftovers)

   1 cup sweet white wine

   2 tablespoons minced shallots

   1 tablespoon saffron threads

   2 egg yolks

   1 cup canola oil

   ½ cup extra-virgin olive oil

   1 teaspoon fresh lemon juice, or more to taste

   Fine sea salt

   White pepper

   3 tablespoons minced chives

In a medium saucepan, combine the wine, shallots, and saffron over medium high heat. Cook until about 2 tablespoons of liquid remain, about 10 minutes. Set aside to cool completely.

In a stand mixer with a whisk attachment, combine the egg yolks and cooled wine reduction. Whisk on medium speed until thoroughly combined, about 30 seconds. Slowly drizzle in the canola oil and olive oil a few teaspoons at a time, alternating between the oils until the mixture begins to thicken. Continue adding oil until the aioli is as thick as mayonnaise (you may not need all the oil). Add the lemon juice and a generous pinch of salt and pepper; mix lightly to combine. Taste and add additional lemon juice, salt, and pepper as needed. Add the chives and mix just to combine. Cover and refrigerate until ready to serve.

White Chocolate Soup with Fresh Berries

This is Josh's favorite easy elegant dessert. "It takes practically no preparation but wows people every time." The key to the dish is getting the berry texture just right, neither frozen solid nor mushy.

Serves 8

- 2 pints assorted berries such as blackberries, raspberries, and blueberries
- 14 ounces good-quality white chocolate such as Lindt or Ghirardelli, chopped
- ¾ to 1 cup heavy cream
- 1 vanilla bean, scraped
- 2 tablespoons finely chopped mint, for garnish

Discard any berries with mold or bruises. Line a shallow baking tray with wax paper and scatter the berries on it. Freeze for 1 hour until icy but not frozen solid (or freeze up to 24 hours and remove from freezer 25 minutes prior to serving).

In the top of a double boiler, melt the chocolate, ¾ cup of the cream, and the vanilla bean over low heat. If the chocolate is too thick, add a little more cream until the mixture is a thick, cream-soup consistency. Remove from the heat and strain into a large serving pitcher. Discard the vanilla bean.

Scatter a few tablespoons of semifrozen berries in the bottom of 8 shallow bowls. At the table pour a small amount of white chocolate into each bowl. Pass the mint separately.

RECIPES

ACKNOWLEDGMENTS

To all the fantastic people—too many to name here—I met while researching this book, thank you for pushing the culinary and entertaining boundaries in such interesting and different ways. It was a pleasure getting to know you as well as dining at your restaurants.

Many thanks to my husband, Kevin, for too many reasons to list. And to mom and dad, Jerre and David Tracy, for realizing that math and science just weren't my thing and for spending your hard-earned money on cobalt blue and titanium white. And to my brother and sister-in-law, Brad and Dawn, for being so darn handy with computer and Web site emergencies (a lifesaver for someone who still wishes she could start each day as Jessica Fletcher, happily typing away on a beat-up Underwood). And many thanks to my mom- and dad-in-law, Linda and Rich, and the entire Garbee family, for never losing that winning-lottery-ticket excitement over every article that has appeared in any publication—amidst constant criticism, so many times it's been exactly what I needed.

And to all my friends who listened ceaselessly to my tales from the underground world, of my constant bouncing around from here to there, and to my warp-speed conversations.

And Danielle Svetcov of Levine Greenberg Literary Agency and Tracy and Emily at Cover to Cover Booksellers in Noe Valley, San Francisco, for planting the seed; and Julie Miller, my fantastic project editor, and Sue Mann, the copy editor. And Susan LaTempa, at the *Los Angeles Times*, for being a mentor in this vast, and sometimes wacky, world of culinary-lifestyle-whatever-else journalism.

Finally, thank you to Gary Luke of Sasquatch Books, and to every other editor who's ever given a first-time author a break.

—Jenn Garbee, June 2008

ABOUT THE AUTHOR

JENN GARBEE is a Santa Monica–based food and travel journalist and professional culinary instructor. She is a regular contributor to the *Los Angeles Times* food and travel sections and a monthly columnist for Tribune Media Services. Her work has been featured in numerous publications including *Robb Report, Chicago Tribune, Baltimore Sun, South Florida Sun-Sentinel, Washington Times,* and on Epicurious.com.

Garbee's interest in cooking goes back to fifth grade show-and-tell, when she offered a classmate raised on Duncan Hines her homemade brownies in exchange for his pet turtle. She took home the turtle.

In 2005, Garbee earned a Diplôme in Le Cordon Bleu Pâtisserie and Baking from the California School of Culinary Arts. Ever since, she's been taking readers to hidden pastry counters, cocktail lounges, wineries, barbeque pits, and underground restaurants nationwide.